APOLLO VERSUS THE ECHOMAKER

A Laingian Approach to Psychotherapy
Dreams and Shamanism

Anthony Lunt was an advanced student of R. D. Laing from 1982 up until Laing's death. He has been in practice as a psychotherapist for twelve years and also writes articles for *International Minds*, a new psychology journal.

Apollo
versus the
Echomaker

A Laingian Approach to Psychotherapy
Dreams and Shamanism

Anthony Lunt

ELEMENT BOOKS

First published in Great Britain in 1990 by
Element Books Limited
Longmead, Shaftesbury, Dorset

Designed by Patrick Knowles
Cover design by Max Fairbrother
Cover illustration by Martin Rieser
Typeset by Butler & Tanner Ltd, Frome and London
Printed and bound in Great Britain by
Billings Ltd, Hylton Road, Worcester

British Library Cataloguing in Publication Data
Lunt, Anthony
Apollo versus the echomaker: a Laingian approach to
psychotherapy, dreams and shamanism.
1. Medicine. Philosophical perspectives
I. Title
610.1

ISBN 1–85230–153–8

For Maria and Anna

Contents

Love, which is divine,
shall inspire thee,
the laws of nature
shall be thy laws.

Paul Tortellier

Introduction

I last met Ronnie Laing the month before he died. We had a wide ranging discussion about his career. Towards the end I asked him how he felt about 'Laingian' now being incorporated into the Oxford English Dictionary? To my complete surprise he replied that he didn't know that it had been, but he was clearly delighted. Ronnie never sought to establish a Laingian school as such. In this way he was like Jung except that Jung did succumb to pressure to do so at the end of his life. Nonetheless, Laingian is an accepted term in the English Language. For me it refers to a particular attitude of mind, and a particular way of being in the world. One aim of this book is to try and make it clear what that attitude of mind is. I have discussed many of these issues with Ronnie during the years that I trained with him. There was nothing that I said about them that he disagreed with.

There are many similarities between Laing and Jung, some of which I draw attention to in this book. Without doubt they were the two most outstanding therapists of their time. There are clear reasons as to why they were both so much greater than their respective contemporaries. One common factor is that neither man saw divisions where others drew them. Unfortunately virtually none of their colleagues have possessed this gift and so see it as a failing. Anthony Storr wrote a scathing and unkind assessment of Laing shortly after he died, in which he wrote that 'Laing also subscribed to a number of other beliefs not generally shared by his colleagues. He also believed in some kind of telepathic link between minds by which gurus could visit their disciples at a distance without physically moving.'[1].

But such things are far from unusual. Storr wrote of Jung

1

'It is easy to lose patience with Jung. More especially I find it difficult to sympathise with his preoccupation with the occult'. As Colin Wilson commented in *Lord of the Under-world*[2], Storr wants to see Jung purely as a scientist, as Freud's greatest successor. But it is a hopeless task. For we have to recognise that, from the very beginning, Jung was obsessed with the occult (the word, after all, means simply 'hidden' ...). Now I find it interesting that someone as pedestrian as Storr should assume that Laing and Jung were the ones to be irritated by. I find it very easy to be irritated by Anthony Storr, particularly when he wrote of Laing at the end of his assessment, 'One is driven to the conclusion that he was not only "much too far out" all his life but that, years ago, he gave up trying to wave to ordinary mortals.'[3] Laing could easily have said like Socrates that 'They would be very loath, I fancy, to admit the truth: which is that they are being convicted of pretending to knowledge when they are entirely ignorant. So, jealous, I suppose, for their own reputation, and also energetic and numerically strong, and provided with a plausible and carefully worked out case against me, these people have been dinning into your ears for a long time past their violent denunciations of myself.'[4]

I shall be eternally grateful to Ronnie Laing for telling me that I am a therapist who was born, not made. I write this book from that standpoint. It will make little sense to those therapists who believe that what they 'know' is more import-ant than how they are. As Blake said, 'One law for the Lion and the Ox is oppression.'

I feel very strongly the terrible gap that has been left by Ronnie's death. I once sent him this poem by Bernard Leach because it was so evocative of time spent with him.

Tea Leaves

You stirred the tea leaves
Before you left last night
Through the dark hours

They would not settle
I could not sleep.

I know that this will be equally true in fifty years' time.

Anthony Lunt
1 Ellesmere Close
Derby Rd
Caversham
Reading

CHAPTER ONE

The First Principle

Then I found myself, or my artistic personality, by looking over my earliest works. They rarely deceive. There I found something that was always the same and which at first glance I thought to be monstrous repetition. It was the work of my personality which appeared the same no matter what different states of mind I happened to have passed through.

I made an effort to develop this personality counting above all on my intuition and by returning again and again to fundamentals.

Henri Matisse[1]

I first became interested in the idea of self-analysis when I was fifteen. At that time I was absolutely dedicated to the idea of becoming a classical guitarist and all my activities were directed to that end. So I began to analyse the way in which my capacity to express emotion was impeded by psychological factors. At first I was more concerned about superficial influences. But as I grew a little older I developed an increasing interest in psychology and psychotherapy.

My teens were not a happy time for me. My mother was mad a lot of the time and regularly took overdoses and my father gave me little indication of feeling any love for me, but repeated indications of hatred and resentment. I left school at eighteen and continued my music studies privately. Some six months' later my mother took a massive overdose and spent the next three months in the local mental hospital. After a short while I began to visit her daily and became very friendly with a number of the patients. This greatly increased my interest in these matters and I began to pursue the whole thing a lot more seriously, as a result of which, some of the anxieties that I was feeling imprisoned by began to ease. My parents divorced when I was nineteen.

The turning point of my life came a year later when I saw, for the second time, a trilogy of television programmes on Jung by Laurens Van der Post. For some reason I had been unaffected by the first showing but the second time around I felt as if I had been struck by lightning and immediately began burying myself in Jung's works. After a while I began to record my dreams and to paint them, as Jung suggested. I rigorously applied Jung's views as I understood them at the time.

In fact dreaming became the most important activity of the day for me. I couldn't wait to go to sleep at night to find out what dreams I would have about the day's experiences. I kept a notebook for my dreams, as I still do, and at that time used a torch so that I wouldn't be woken up too much if I wrote them down in the night. I thought things were going pretty well until I had the following dream.

I was in my bedroom. My French teacher came in to see what work I had done. He left and I looked at what I had written in the dream book that he had been looking at. It was impossible to read. I then realised that I had to hold the book up to the mirror on a dressing table in the bedroom and shine a light on it. After various contortions I could suddenly see what was written in the book. It was one word, in very large letters, (which I can still see as vividly as when I dreamed it) – NESCIENCE.

NESCIENCE is a state of ignorance. As you might imagine I found this deeply humiliating. It came as a real shock and very much undermined my confidence. However, I continued to read Jung avidly – assuming that the fault lay with my not understanding Jung sufficiently.

Some months later I spent a long sleepless night. I only got about an hour's sleep because I was waiting for something to happen. I had no idea what it was but eventually it emerged as two brief dreams. The first was of two fish rushing around in a circle trying to bite each others' tails and neither succeeding. I took this to relate to my attempts at analysing myself — that I was going round and round in circles not getting anywhere.

The second dream, though, had enormous feeling to it. It consisted of a brief glimpse of a benign yet frightening Merlin figure dressed entirely in black. To his left was a large Chinese gong and in his right hand was a large stick with a large globe at the end with which he beat the gong. The figure then stood stock still and said 'Turn away from me for I am the Echo Maker.'

At that time I had only ever written about ten poems but I was so affected by this dream that I wrote the following poem about it entitled, 'I meet the Echo Maker'.

Frightened he turned away
The withered plant — his soul
The beautiful flower — his imagination.
Here, curtained from the darkness of the night sky
    the Echo Maker struck another note. Stick in hand
    he screamed,
His piercing laugh echoed the desperate dance
    between man and silence.
A dance to the death.
'Turn away from me', he screamed.
'Turn away from me, for I am the Echo Maker.'

Although I continued to read Jung and to apply his ideas, the grip that he had upon me began to diminish and this dream had a lot to do with it. It was a clear message that I had to find my own voice and stop being an echo of someone else.

The Merlin figure was significant too because, prior to the Jung programme, I had written a number of discussions between a wise old man and a youth and it was in particular learning about Jung's account of what he called the archetype of the wise old man that had so strongly drawn me to him. So to have such a figure standing in my way in the dream and saying I had to turn away from him was immensely significant to me.

Within another year I had left home and, encouraged by the girlfriend I had at the time, decided to move into psychotherapy as a career. It took me some time to decide where to train. I eventually chose somewhere and commenced the therapy that I had to undergo before I could be accepted for training. At the beginning of the treatment I had the following dream.

I was in an army training school – my father was there – and I saw some recruits in some sort of an exercise. I decided to join them. I had scarcely done so when a large round bomb fell down in front of me and my brains were blown out of my head. I then thought that wasn't acceptable and so rewound the dream, so to speak, to a point before the bomb fell – the dream continued as before. But this time when the bomb made its appearance, I knew what was going to happen and quickly searched for a means of escape but there appeared to be none. Suddenly I found myself floating up into the air. The whole ambiance of the dream now changed. I realised that the only solution was for me to conceive myself. I changed into a Christ-like figure but one that was involved in a sort of orgasm that was due to his creating himself. An extraordinary light glowed over the whole scene. In addition, the Sanctus from Bach's *Mass in B Minor* thundered out. I carried on rising until I landed on top of a cliff – high above where I had come from.

This dream obsessed me for a very long time to come, in fact I continue to be fascinated by it and to find other ways of giving meaning to it. Within the context we are discussing, however, the central feature that it pointed out was the need for me to create myself. From that point of view the dream was already an unfavourable comment upon the therapy I was receiving at the time. Even though the training course that I had embarked upon at the Psychotherapy Centre in

London claimed to be non-theoretical and *eclectic*, which is why I had chosen it, and even though it was claimed that the patient was helped to find his own solutions to problems, that actually was very far from the case.

Some months later I dreamed what is, to date, the most important dream of my life.

I am with a number of people in a museum. It is poorly lit. We are all searching for the key to the unconscious. Some people have been searching for a very long time without success. Suddenly I find the key. It is lying on top of the bare earth – in a museum case.

I find this dream profoundly moving. The more time passes, the more it means to me. In a sense, though, the dream is like a Zen statement; for those who understand it no explanation is needed, but it is rather something to meditate upon.

On a purely practical basis the dream has acted like a lodestone. The more time passes, the more I realise that it is unnecessary to think in terms of digging deep into the unconscious in order to find the clues, as Freud had believed. On the contrary, everything you need to know is on the surface, provided that you can see it.

Later I had a patient who dreamed of the two of us looking at pebbles and stones through water – she had resumed therapy with me after a years' interval – and said that whereas before, the feeling of the therapy had been one of digging, now she felt it to be like picking up the pebbles that were easily to be seen on the bottom of the stream.

The fact that the first dream that I had when I began training was of my being in an army training school, shows the extent to which I had unconsciously realised at the outset what the reality of training there was to be. Despite their intellectual protestations of encouraging independent thinking, the reality was very different and this applied even more when one went into practice. Eventually, after working there for four years, I left on a question of principle.

I continually felt doubts about the way that I had been

trained to conduct myself as a psychotherapist. The basic approach was very heavily influenced by the classic psychoanalytic setup. The patient lay on a couch. I sat in a chair behind them, out of sight, refusing to answer personal questions, refusing to give advice. One analyst of this persuasion praised Melanie Klein for her impeccable technique, saying that Klein never said 'hello' when the patient arrived for a session, or 'goodbye' when they left! Well I was never that bad although like all 'self respecting' therapists I never accepted presents from patients. However I was always very unhappy with the traditional notion that I had been trained with, that any love that the patient felt towards me had nothing to do with myself but was a transference onto me of feelings to do with their parents. It seemed natural to me that if I were the person that my patient had felt most safe with, and able to talk to and be honest with, and that if I helped them to fulfil themselves and to get out of life what before they had only dreamed of, then they would feel love towards me and I for them. Nonetheless I couldn't imagine having any social contact with patients and all forms of physical contact were avoided like the plague. In short I was trained to have a totally paranoid attitude towards the people who were coming to me for help. The classic psychoanalytic arrangement really only suits someone who is terrified of human beings. In fact Freud, who was an intensely shy man, once admitted that he had his patients lying on a couch because he couldn't abide being stared at for ten hours a day.

The whole experience is as dehumanised as is possible to imagine. I am just appalled at the distress I created for a number of my patients while I blithely congratulated myself on my classic technique.

I remember the first dent in my thinking along these lines came when I made an appointment to see Dr Denys Kelsey, who practised near Pangbourne. When I phoned him he offered to give me a lift from the station because I did not have a car. I was so shocked at this suggestion that I thought there must be something seriously wrong with him. It was

only when we were actually driving along that I realised how
natural it was and how unnatural my attitude had been.

The next big shock came when I started to train with
Laing and to see him as a patient, and I asked him a question
that he couldn't answer without revealing something about
himself. I asked it fully expecting him either to say nothing
at all as my previous training therapist would have done or
to turn the question back on me. But I thought, 'what the
hell' and asked anyway and was completely flummoxed when
he unhesitatingly answered it. 'My God,' I thought, 'something isn't right here'. What wasn't right was the attitude I'd
been trained to adopt, that normal human interactions have
no part in psychotherapy. This really is a paradox; that
analysts should be attempting to help their patients to behave
in ways that are outlawed in the consulting room. It is a
travesty that most analysts take the view that even when a
patient is 'cured', the therapist can never socialise with them.
Whatever theories are used to justify this attitude it seems
to me to be a blatant expression of the acute paranoia that
underlies so much of the practice of psychotherapy. One of
the basic tenets of the Laingian approach to psychiatry and
psychotherapy is that one should treat the patient with the
same courtesy and friendliness one would anyone else.

If the word 'neurotic' has to be used, then I feel very
strongly that the use of 'technique' by a therapist is neurotic.
A therapist should behave or respond as he does because he
feels it is the most appropriate action to take in the situation.
It cannot work if a therapist feels he has to use his 'technique'
to help his patients be more natural and spontaneous.

Everything in therapy should be as natural as possible.
Other than the question of payment, the only major difference
between the relationship the patient has with the therapist
and his other relationships is that he is asked, in so far as he
can, to say what comes into his mind. When people ask me
to describe therapy I say that the patient says what comes
into his mind and I have to do the same. I have learnt by
hard experience to give expression to even the silliest

thoughts that come into my mind – in fact it is often the silliest or the oddest that are most relevant. Honesty is as necessary for the mind as oxygen is for the body.

The therapists responsibility is to provide a mental space for the patient to be able to be honest in. But it isn't just a question of providing the space, but of its quality. In many respects the quality of that space reflects the quality of the therapist. Laing is the only truly great therapist that I have encountered other than Jung, who I never met. So what was the quality that made them great?

The best account that I have come across is in *Casals and The Art of Interpretation*, by Blum. It comes at the start of Chapter One which is headed with this quote from Casals which applies as much to the therapists as it does to musicians. *Technique, wonderful sound ... all of this is sometimes astounding – but it is not enough.*

Blum then wrote: 'As Western students of Oriental culture have discovered, the First Principle does not lend itself to precise translation,' said my Chinese friend, an art historian. 'It is something definite, yet it is indescribable. It is how you feel when you enter a room and sense that everything in it is somehow harmonious; you know that you are at peace there. It is how your life suddenly seems to change when you fall in love. It is the way in which your spirit comes in subtle accord with the movement of life around you; at the same time it is an experience within yourself – at the very centre. It is active and passive, embracing and releasing; it is a profound sense of being.'[2]

From the first moment that Laing sat down I felt that I had come home.

'We were discussing Ch'i-Yun, the first of the Six Principles set down by the art critic Hseih Ho in the fifth century AD in what is thought to be the earliest document stating the fundamental canons of Chinese painting. It was maintained that in order to become a master, the artist must prove himself in the following skills: vitality of brush stroke, accuracy in portrayal, versatility in colouring, care in arrangement of composition, transmission of tradition through copying the works of the earliest masters. But the foremost task lay in the fulfillment of the First Principle, which has sometimes been defined as "breath-resonance life-motion." For only by coming into harmony with the vital cosmic spirit or breath could the painter convey through the movement of his brush the mysterious vitality of life itself.'

It was this vitality that I felt Laing had in plenty.

To my mind Freud's most important contribution to the practice of psychotherapy was his urging of the therapist not to focus his mind on what the patient is saying but rather to allow himself 'free-floating attention', that is, to put the conscious mind to one side and to listen with the unconscious. 'From the heart to the heart', as Beethoven wrote on one of his manuscripts. It is the successful capacity to use free-floating attention that creates the opportunity for the therapist to acquire and embody the First Principle and thereby to allow his unconscious intuitive faculties to operate. This was the essence of Laing's approach to therapy.

Unfortunately, in the West intuition comes low down in the scale of values that have been established by the influence of scientific materialism and the high precedence that it places upon so-called 'objectivity'. This holds true despite the fact that so many major advances in science have been made through the use, or should I say, the experience of intuition. The proper attitude towards a patient – that of free-floating attention, can only operate if the therapist trusts that his unconscious will provide him with meaningful responses to what is said and to what takes place.

Such a stance lies at the heart of much of the thinking and culture of the East – particularly in Japan, where these issues are discussed with an understanding that puts our psychology to shame – not only discussed but also put into practice, for instance in the application of Zen to the arts and the martial arts.

In 1972 the great potter, Bernard Leach, adapted the writings of his close friend, Soetsu Yanagi, and produced a book that is a Japanese aesthetic. He called it *The Unknown Craftsman*.[3] I regard it as the most important book on art and craft ever written – its implications are enormously far-reaching. Yanagi expresses himself so well that I will quote extensively from him. So much of what he says is directly relevant to the practice of psychotherapy and explains why the adoption of free-floating attention is so important.

Yanagi gets to the very heart of the matter in his essay *Seeing and Knowing*. It is important to remember that everything he has to say about seeing applies equally to listening. It is curious how listening itself is not a subject that is addressed in training courses for psychotherapy. It should never be taken for granted that a therapist knows how to listen in the way that Yanagi writes of and yet if he cannot, much of what is truly important and unique in the patient will be missed. To feel the relevance of this passage one can substitute the word 'people' for the word 'beauty'. Yanagi begins: –

Being and knowing are often separate. Nothing could be more admirable than when they coincide, but only too often they remain estranged. In some fields this does not matter, but in the areas of aesthetic or art history or the like, any gap between perception and knowledge assumes fatal proportions. This is an obvious fact that is too frequently overlooked. Similar cases are common in other fields as well. The critic of religion, for example, who has no religious feelings has no force in his criticisms. In the same way, the moralist who does not live by his theories carries no weight however brilliant he may be. I know many famous art critics who have no feeling of beauty and I cannot therefore respect their knowledge. They may be learned but it avails nothing. It is the same with philosophy and history. The student of philosophy and the philosopher should be distinguished; a man who knows a great deal about history is not necessarily an historian.

Doubtless many would reply that intuitive perception of beauty is incomplete without learning, that
without knowledge one does not see a thing as a whole.
Socrates saw the identity of action and knowing. To see
and at the same time to comprehend is the idea, but in
practice we are far removed from this unity. The things
to be seen and the knowledge to be gained have so
vastly increased in this modern age that man's activities
have been pushed either into one direction or the other.
But of the two, those forced into the field of knowledge
are in the worst position as far as beauty is concerned.

To be unable to see beauty properly is to lack the
basic foundation of any aesthetic understanding. One
should refrain from becoming a student of aesthetics
just because one has a good brain; to know a lot about
beauty is no qualification. Seeing and knowing form an
exterior, not a right and a left. Either way, they are not
equal. In understanding beauty, intuition is more of the
essence than intellectual perception.

The reversal of these two faculties stultified vision.
To 'see' is to go direct to the core; to know the facts
about an object of beauty is to go around the periphery.
Intellectual discrimination is less essential to an understanding of beauty than the power of intuition that
precedes it.

Beauty is a kind of mystery, which is why it cannot
be grasped by the intellect. The part of it available to
the intellect lacks depth. He who only knows, without
seeing, does not understand the mystery. Even should
every detail of beauty be accounted for by the intellect,
does such a tabulation lead to beauty? Is the beauty that
can be neatly reckoned really profound? The scholar of
aesthetics tends to base his ideas on knowledge – or
rather, he tries to make seeing proceed from knowing.
But this is a reversal of the natural order of things.

The eye of knowledge cannot, thereby, see beauty.
What is the beauty that a man of erudition sees as he

holds a fine pot in his hands? If he picks a wild flower
to pieces petal by petal and counts them and tries to
put them together again, can he regain the beauty that
was there? All the assembly of dead parts cannot bring
life again. It is the same with knowing. One cannot
replace the function of seeing by the function of
knowing. One may be able to turn intuition into knowledge, but one cannot produce intuition out of knowledge. This is the basis of aesthetics, [therapy] must not
be intellectual concepts. . . .

Seeing is a born faculty, knowledge is acquired. To
a point anyone can acquire knowledge, but the potential
of seeing is born within us. Although some are more
gifted than others, it is generally accepted that the
musical or the artistic gifts are born with us and that
there is nothing to be done about it if one is not so
fortunate. The gift of seeing is of the same order. This
leaves the ungifted forlorn. I would like to give them
three pieces of advice. [All psychotherapists please note].

First put aside the desire to judge immediately;
acquire the habit of just looking, second, do not treat
the object as an object of intellect. Third, just be ready
to receive, passively, without interposing yourself. If
you can void your mind of all intellectualization, like a
clear mirror that simply reflects, all the better. This non-
conceptualization – the Zen state of mushin ('no mind') –
may seem to represent a negative attitude, but from it
springs the true ability to contact things directly and
positively.

This final paragraph is the clearest statement that I can
imagine of Laing's behaviour as a psychotherapist and it
encapsulates everything that I seek to achieve in myself.

At one time Laing suggested that one should practise a
form of meditation which 'looks at the phenomena before
one, just as they are, wherever one is, and does not make

any particular thing out of them: but simply pays attention to whatever it is.'

David Blum quotes Casals as saying: – 'Real understanding does not come from what we learn in books; it comes from what we learn from love – love of nature, of music, of man. For only what is learned in that way is truly understood.'[4]

This is very similar to Laing's statement in *The Divided Self*. 'The personalities of Doctor and psychotic, no less than the personalities of expositor and author, do not stand opposed to each other as two external facts that do not meet and cannot be compared. Like the expositor, the therapist must have the plasticity to transpose himself into another strange and even alien view of the world. In this act, he draws on his own psychotic possibilities, without foregoing his sanity. Only thus can he arrive at any understanding of the patients existential position.'[5]

Laing then continues along the same lines as Casals: 'I think it is clear that by "understanding" I do not mean a purely intellectual process. For understanding one might say love.' And later in the same work Laing states that: 'The main agent in uniting the patient, in allowing the pieces to come together and cohere, is the physicians love, a love that recognises the patients total being, and accepts it, with no strings attached.'[6]

Leonard Bernstein, in his book *Findings* also says something that is very germane to this point. 'I believe in man's unconscious, the deep spring from which comes his power to communicate and to love. For me, all art is a combination of these powers, art is nothing to me if it does not make contact between the creator and the perceiver on an unconscious level. Let us say that love is the way we have of communicating personally in the deepest way.'[7]

It is shocking how rarely the word love is used in this sense, in the analytical literature, particularly with reference to the therapist's feelings and attitudes towards his patients. One can read dozens of books and never find it mentioned as anything other than a manifestation of the patients, or worse still the therapist's neurosis.

Laing once said, 'But human life is only dust and ashes without love. If you investigate and enquire into the world without love, you don't find anything worthwhile, you obtain only heartless knowledge.'[8]

I agree with all the statements quoted above. Many people in therapy and particularly those with serious difficulties will not be cured of their problems unless the therapist is able to provide them with the love and understanding that was missing in their childhood. This doesn't mean that he has to be chocolate boxey or lovey-dovey with them. But it does mean that he should have a sense of deep concern and interest in the person as he actually is rather than as the therapist would like him to be. And this too most certainly does not mean that the therapist should not feel that he can't dislike aspects of his patient or get angry with him if these are appropriate responses to his patient's behaviour.

At this point I must emphasise that I only make reference to the idea of the therapist as parent with regard to the individual receiving the sort of attention from his therapist that he should have done from his parents. But the same stance from one person to another should apply as much in friendship or a love relationship as between parent and child. It is certainly not my intention to suggest that the therapist should see himself as his patient's parent. Although some therapists, notably Ferenzie, have done so. On the contrary, as Jung said in *Problems of Modern Psychotherapy*: '... the Doctor is as much "in the analysis" as the patient. He is equally a part of the psychic process of treatment and therefore equally exposed to the transforming influences. Indeed, to the extent that the Doctor shows himself impervious to this influence, he forfeits influence over the patient, and if he is influenced only unconsciously, there is a gap in his field of consciousness which makes it impossible for him to see the patient in true perspective ... The Doctor is therefore faced with the same task which he wants his patient to face.'[9]

Laing has given the best description of psychotherapy as
I understand it in the following passage from *The Politics of
Experience*. 'In the practice of psychotherapy, the very diver-
sities of method have made the essential simplicity more
clear.

'The irreducible elements of psychotherapy are a therapist, a patient and a regular and reliable time and place. But
given these, it is not easy for two people to meet. We all live
on the hope that authentic meeting between human beings
can still occur. Psychotherapy consists of the paring away of
all that stands between us, the props, masks, roles, lies,
defences, anxieties, projections and introjections, in short,
all the carry-overs from the past, transference and counter-
transference, that we use by habit and collusion, wittingly or
unwittingly, as our currency for relationships. It is this
currency, these very media, that re-create and intensify the
conditions of alienation that originally occasioned them.'[10]

In his book *Gandhi the Man*, Eknath Easwaran wrote,
'very few of us see life as it is. Most of us see things only as
we are looking at others through our own likes and dislikes,
prejudices and prepossessions, desires, interests and fears. It's
the separatists outlook that fragments life for us — person
against person, community against community, nation
against nation. In order to see life as it is, one undivided
whole, we have to shed all attachment to personal profit,
power, pleasure or prestige. Otherwise we cannot help
looking at life through our individual conditions and we will
see the world not as it is but as conditioned by our desires.'[11]

A few weeks before he died Ronnie Laing agreed to my
interviewing him for a book on Citizens of the World. During
the interview he described the sort of thing that people all
over the world, particularly patients who came into contact
with him, said; 'They say "you've given me permission to be
and you don't seem to be playing any numbers on me. Do
you realise, Dr Laing, how rare that is? I've gone to see
twenty people or one hundred people and believe me I'm
telling you, I've never met anybody like you — who's not

making any numbers. You let me be and you understand me – not making a big deal about seeming to understand me. So thank you Dr Laing, just for being." '

Let us see how this approach can be applied to the mode of experience that we call dreaming. We can then see how far removed conventional psychoanalysis is from this stance and how that necessarily limits the type of experience that people are able to undergo in such therapy.

CHAPTER TWO

Dreams

Listen to your own inner voice and go your own
modest but sure way. You won't be any the worse
for that.

Sibelius.

From the moment that a child is born he will, if he is lucky,
have parents who relate to him more in terms of his needs
than of their own. As parents they will be more concerned
with what he is trying to communicate than with what they
wish to hear, more delighted by how he actually is than
determined to see him, and make him, into the image of what
they want him to be.

Such a child, providing that his parents haven't been
too self-effacing, should develop into an adult who is both
cognisant of and interested in the views and arguments of
others and yet confident enough to arrive at his own conclusions and to live his life on the basis of them. He will show
the same respect for the right of others to have their own
views that his parents had shown to him, and he will derive
little pleasure from intellectually bullying others into accept-
ing his viewpoint.

It is rare for someone who seeks psychotherapy to have
had this experience. Most of my patients have either suffered
from obvious neglect or from that more insidious form of
neglect which results from the parents relating, not to the
child, but to the image they have of him.

They love the child they imagine to be there and are
devoted to him and do everything for him but they neglect
the real human being that they pin their projections onto.
Such children often develop into adults with what I call

chameleon personalities – they take on the colour of their surroundings. You can see them at parties and bus stops not daring to say anything until they think they know what the other person wants them to say. Put two chameleons together and they will invariably say nothing at all but sit or stand in painful silence.

When a person with this sort of problem comes into therapy they will often do so on the basis that I will tell them how to be or what to do in order for their problems to go away. Their attitude towards the treatment and their experiences of it are themselves a reflection of their difficulties. In other words they want me to be like their parents. But clearly if I fitted in with this outlook I wouldn't be helping them to escape their difficulties although they may experience some relief from having me telling them what they are and what I think they should be. On the other hand, hearing my views may be a starting point for them to develop their own.

A person with such a background is obviously going to be in trouble if he can't accept his parents injunctions because the way in which they have related to him will have made it difficult or impossible for him to think for himself. He will be likely to feel that his existence is meaningless and is very likely to ask me at some point what the meaning of life is.

We can never know what life means or even if it has a meaning, but we can give life a meaning. The majority have been prepared to accept the meaning that others, such as religious or political leaders and thinkers, have given to life. But some individuals are unable to do so and they have then to set about constructing their own sense of what life means. There are many people who assume that the meaning which they give to life or that they accept as having been given to life, corresponds to the meaning of life, but this is pure prejudice because even if they were right there is no way of their proving that they are, either to themselves or to others.

Much the same situation exists where dreams are concerned. We don't discover the meaning of a dream – we give it a meaning. Because we are consciously entirely outside

the process by which a dream is created we are in no position
to say that we know what a dream means or even if it has a
meaning. As Jung said, we assume that dreams are meaningful.
A patient may feel that what I say a dream means to me is
of more value to him than what it means to himself, but that
is not to say that I am right.

Of course some dreams do seem to be very transparent
and obvious. For instance, a woman in her early sixties came
to consult me. For the previous seventeen years she had slept
on a couch in the front room of her sister's flat. Having no
life of her own she was totally dominated by this sister and
their aged mother. She hadn't experienced intercourse for
twenty three years; the man she had loved from afar had
been murdered. She felt no hope of finding any happiness
and repeatedly dreamed that she had missed the bus, an
image that accurately depicted how she felt about life. The
dream haunted her so remorselessly that she felt compelled
to seek help to wipe away that Dorian Grey portrait of her
failure. Fortunately, she was able to resolve her problems
sufficiently to get her own flat and to have a full sexual
relationship with a man who meant a great deal to her.

There is a very important passage in Jung's autobiography, *Memories, Dreams and Reflections*, that seems
invariably to go unnoticed – certainly I have never seen a
reference to it in any of the literature on Jung. He wrote,
'After the parting of the ways with Freud a period of inner
uncertainty began for me. It would be no exaggeration to
call it a state of disorientation. I felt totally suspended in mid-
air for I had not yet found my footing. Above all I felt it
necessary to develop a new attitude towards my patients. I
resolved for the present not to bring any theoretical premises
to bear upon them but to wait and see what they would tell
of their own accord. My aim became to leave things to
chance. The result was that the patients would spontaneously
report their dreams and fantasies to me and I would merely
ask, "What occurs to you in connection with that?" or, "How
do you mean that, where does that come from, what do you

think about it?" The interpretations seemed to follow of their own accord from the patients' replies and associations. I avoided all theoretical points of view and simply helped the patients to understand the dream-images by themselves, without application of rules and theories.'

Jung continued, 'Soon I realised that it was right to take the dreams in this way as the basis of interpretation, for that is how dreams are intended. They are the facts from which we must proceed'. Unfortunately, he then added, 'Naturally, the aspects resulting from this method were so multitudinous that the need for a criteria grew more and more pressing — the need, I might almost put it, for some initial orientation.'[1]

I say 'unfortunately' because I can see nothing natural in Jung's need for a criteria. Why did he feel a pressing need for some initial orientation when his patients were (by his own account) doing perfectly well without Jung feeling orientated? If he had had an artistic rather than a scientific training, I'm not so sure that he would have done so.

The inability to tolerate a sense of intellectual disorientation took Jung, in my view, in some respects further away from the truth rather than towards it, although it did lead to his discovery of archetypal patterns. By 'truth' I mean the patients sense of inner truth. And here I agree completely with Alfred Reynolds when he wrote in *Pilates Question*[2] 'The personality begins with its grasp of, and commitment to, personal truth and how this awareness of truth becomes the decisive factor in its growth.'

In the Tavistock lectures Jung rightly said, 'above all we should avoid speculation and theories, when we have to deal with such mysterious processes as dreams'

The way that can be spoken of
  Is not the constant way,
The name that can be named
  Is not the constant name.
                    Lao Tzu[3]

Just as an individual may feel happier abdicating personal

responsibility for creating his own sense of what life means
to him and prefer to accept the meaning that others give, so
too may a patient prefer to accept the meaning that others
give to his dreams rather than arriving at his own understanding of them. Some approaches to therapy encourage
this dependency.

In his *Introductory Lectures on Psychoanalysis* Freud wrote,
'I have already admitted to you that it does sometimes really
happen that nothing occurs to a person under analysis in
response to particular elements of his dreams. It is true that
this does not happen as often as he asserts; in a great many
cases, with perseverance, an idea is extracted from him. But
nevertheless there remain cases in which an association fails
to emerge or, if it is extracted *does not give us what we expected
from it.*'[4] (My italics).

This last point gives the lie to Freud's attitude towards
his patients' dreams – that what he is interested in is his
patient saying what he expects them to, that is, he is only
satisfied if the meaning that they give to a dream corresponds
to the meaning that he gives to it.

Freud continued, 'If this happens during a psycho-analytic
treatment it has a peculiar significance with which we are not
here concerned.' The plot thickens – if you can't give the
meaning to the dream that Freud expects you to, then you
are resisting!

'In this way we are tempted to interpret these 'mute'
dream elements ourselves to set about translating them with
our own resources.' This is fine in so far as it goes, in that
Freud's acknowledging that he gives his own meaning to the
dream. But then follows a statement that is shockingly naive
and stupid:- 'We are then forced to recognise that whenever
we venture on a replacement of this sort we arrive at a
satisfactory sense for the dream, whereas it remains senseless
and the chain of thought is interrupted so long as we refrain
from interfering in this way.'

So what Freud is now saying is that if his patient can't
say what a dream means to them then he, Freud, will say

what meaning he gives to the dream and having done that he is then 'forced to admit' that the meaning that he has given to it makes sense to him! Matters get worse as one piece of illogical thinking is piled onto another:- 'An accumulation of many similar cases eventually gives the necessary certainty to what began as a timid experiment.'

Let us create an example — Freud was fond of thinking that an umbrella in a dream represented a penis. A penis was what an umbrella meant to him. If a number of people dream of umbrellas and each time Freud says that the umbrella represents a penis (the accumulation of many cases) then he is now certain that he is right.

'In this way we obtain constant translation [of course] for a number of dream elements — just as popular dream books provide them for everything that appears in dreams. There is, however, something further. For when with experience we have collected enough of these constant renderings, the time comes when we realise that we should in fact have been able to deal with these portions of dream interpretation from our own knowledge and that they could really be understood without the dreamers associations. How it is that we must necessarily have known their meaning will become clear. A constant relation of this kind between a dream element and its translation is described by us as a "symbolic one" and the dream element itself as a symbol of the unconscious dream thought.'

It is hard to imagine a worse example of circular thinking — what in philosophy is called petitio principii, taking for granted a premis which itself depends upon the conclusion that one is trying to prove.

Freud used faulty thinking to put himself in a position where he identifies what a dream meant to him with 'knowing' what the dream means. His use of the word 'knowledge' is seductive and persuasive as circular arguments often are because it begs the question of whether his assumption is correct. In the end Freud believed that he didn't need the dreamer to tell him anything about what the dream meant to them. Freud put his patients into the totally false position that they had come to him to get them out of. Hence, Kraus's condemnation of psychoanalysis as being the illness of which it purports to be the cure.

Anna Faraday described what it is like to undergo this sort of experience of analysis in her book *Dream Power*:- 'My reaction was and still is that violence has been done to the dream and to my psyche, which produced it. I felt that my analyst had not listened to me at all but had interpreted the dream according to some preconceived ideas about women and Freudian dream theory. I am angry that I allowed myself to be led away from my own train of thought by red herrings which obviously interested my analyst but had little reference to me.'[5]

Faraday's account of her analyst's attitude and behaviour towards her corresponds exactly to the bad pattern of parenting that I described at the start of this chapter. All too often, it seems to me, therapists use theories as a means to justify re-enacting with their patients the experiences that their parents imposed upon them as children. In 1919 Freud stated 'at the present time theoretical knowledge is still far more important to all of us than therapeutic success.'

In his book, *The First Interview with a Psychiatrist*, Berg unwit-tingly illustrates the vast divide that exists between himself and his patients. One patient said to him 'I have had a hell of a life, owing to this conflict in me created by my parents (I know that you will not have that).' Berg denied the validity of the patient's comments saying 'there appears to be a strong bias on the part of people suffering from psychoneurosis to blame their parents for their illness.' Another patient said, 'It was the unhappiness all through my childhood, owing to my feelings that they did not love me, which produced the tension and it was the tension that produced the habit.' Berg commented that, 'Analysis reveals that this quarrel with the parents is a regressive projection (or regression of the conflict between id and super ego), the intrapsychic conflict behind every psychoneurosis.' Hardly surprising that one patient shouted at him 'Shut up! You have tried too many interpretations and not allowed me enough free wheeling.'

It is chilling to contemplate how far Berg was removed from the reality of his patients' experience, so obsessed was he with the intellectual concepts that he had picked up from Freud. This is the very opposite of the Laingian approach which involves one person, the therapist, trying to understand another person, the patient, using the patient's terms of reference.

It is significant that a physician who studies and treats mental illness is known as an 'alienist' and the study and treatment of mental illness is known as 'alienism'. The nomenclature is remarkably apt where Berg is concerned because not only does he see his patients as alien in the sense of 'foreign' or 'different in nature' by describing them as psychoneurotic but he 'alienates' the patient in its sense as a transitive verb meaning 'to divert'. He diverts attention from the patient to a theory, from an emotional to an intellectual level. Significantly too, as a transitive verb alienate can also mean 'to estrange' (to put a stop to affection), which reminds me of Dr Peter Parish's statement (Supplement No 4 Vol 21 (No 92) of the Journal of the Royal College of General Practitioners) 'But the increasing prescribing of CNS (central nervous system) depressant drugs suggests that general practitioners are blanketing their patients' emotional reactions to an excessive degree and they must ask themselves whether it is right for them to produce a pharmacological leucotomy in contemporary society.'

One can argue that alienation is intrinsic to Freud's theory of dreams in that it is the central tenet of his approach to dreams. 'We must not concern ourselves with what the dream appears to tell us, whether it is intelligible or absurd, clear or confused, since it cannot possibly be the unconscious material we are in search of.'[6]

Again Freud knows what he wants to hear – he assumes that what he wants to hear is what the patient needs to say (a bit worrying when the same Freud once said 'I always find it uncanny when I can't understand someone in terms of myself'). So even if the dream makes complete sense to the patient as it stands, as for instance in the case of the 'missing the bus' dream – it can't be what he is in search of. Freud called the dream as remembered, the manifest content and the thoughts that he believed it related to, the latent content. He argued that the manifest dream content contained a number of means of concealing the latent dream thoughts. As a matter of interest Jung argued strongly against this proposition of Freud's.

There is an obvious danger here that Freud can argue that the dream means whatever he wants it to mean, particularly when one couples this with his thinking on dream symbolism and the idea that he doesn't need the patient's associations at all in order to be able to interpret these elements of the dream. The standard text on the definitions of psychoanalysis is *The Psychoanalytic Theory of the Neuroses* by Fenichel. In this work Fenichel wrote that the procedure of deducing what the patient actually means and telling it to him is called interpretation. This condescending approach is worrying – the patient does not know what he means, the analyst has to tell him! – again, precisely the parental attitude that creates such difficulties for a child and yet this very attitude is supposedly used to overcome these effects.

It would be difficult to argue that Pablo Picasso was a paragon of mental health but when he said about young painters that 'The important thing is that they start out with what belongs to them, is in them, and not with that which belongs to others or with what others discovered', he expressed a far greater understanding of what is the precondition for growth than a lot of psychoanalysts.

A dream of my own points to the limitations that arise from applying Freud's approach to dreams. A few years ago I dreamed that I was near the top of a tree in a wood. Looking down I saw two teenage girls with their mother. One of the girls was dressed in jogging clothes. They needed my help and I started to descend the tree in order to help them. The scene changed to a room with a table and chairs in. Sitting at the table was the same woman. I was furious with her and slammed her head down on the table. She jolted back but now there was a terrible look on her face and I was terrified that she was dead. The scene changed again to my being across the road looking at the building in which the woman was, watching people going in and out; I realised that she was okay.

I regularly analyse my dreams first thing in the morning and was really quite shaken by this one, particularly the ghostly sight of the woman's face. While making a drink and wondering what on earth could be the reason for having such an awful dream, there was a knock on the door. It was a teenage girl who I hadn't seen before, dressed in a jogger's outfit. She turned out to be a neighbour and was in a desperate state, begging me to come to her house to help her mother. In the house was her sister and in the kitchen — which I had never seen before but was exactly as I had dreamt — the woman I dreamt of was slumped in a chair, a ghastly look fixed on her face. I felt convinced she was dying. They asked me to help them move her — which I did — and then, since they made it clear that they wanted to be alone with her, I returned to my house, went upstairs and looked out of the window towards their property. As there were a large number of trees in the garden the view was very similar to that from the tree in the first part of my dream. An ambulance arrived, she was brought out, and I could then see she hadn't died.

Although there are some disparities between my dream and the actual event, the correspondences are far more numerous and certainly far more meaningful to myself. Take away what Freud called the manifest content of the dream and you destroy the whole experience — an experience that had a profound effect upon me.

In one of his most significant statements, hidden away in a letter Jung wrote, 'Science is the art of creating suitable illusions which the fool believes or argues against, but the wise man enjoys their beauty or their ingenuity without being blind to the fact that they are human veils and curtains concealing the abysmal darkness of the unknowable.'[7]

The whole idea of a scientific approach to dreams is naive and destructive towards the human experience to which it is being applied. Why this is necessarily so, has been brilliantly set out by Vaihinger in *The Philosophy of 'As If'*:- 'The factor common to all fictions in this class consists of a neglect of important elements of reality. As a rule the reason for the formation of these fictions is to be sought in the highly intricate character of the facts which make theoretical treatment exceedingly difficult owing to their unusual complexity. The logical functions are thus unable to perform their work undisturbed because it is not possible here to keep the various threads out of which reality is woven apart from one another. Since, then, the material is too complicated and confused for thought to be able to break it up into its component elements, and since the causal factors sought are probably of too complicated a nature for them to be determined directly, thought makes use of an artifice by means of which it provisionally and temporarily neglects a number of characters and selects from them the more important phenomena.

The empirical manifestations of human actions are so excessively complicated that they present almost insuperable obstacles when we try to understand them theoretically, and to reduce them to causal factors.'[8]

It is precisely in the act of selecting the 'important phenomena' that the therapist or patient is giving meaning to an experience or action rather than finding the meaning of it. But the situation outlined by Vaihinger shouldn't be cause for despondence because some form of certainty is not required in order for people to resolve their difficulties and to grow.

To return to Vaihinger for a moment: 'It is a universal phenomenon of nature that means which serve a purpose often undergo a more complete development than is necessary for the attainment of their purpose ... This Preponderance of the Means over the End has also taken place in thought, which in the course of time has gradually lost sight of its original practical purpose and is finally practised for its sake as theoretical thought. As a result this thought which appears to be independent and theoretical in its origins, sets itself problems which are impossible, not only to human thought but to every form of thought, for instance, the problems of the origin and meaning of the universe.'[9] This is precisely what Freud did and is the error that underlies all theoretically based approaches to psychotherapy.

As opposed to this I propose the following empirical statement:- 'It is not the therapist's knowledge or supposed knowledge that cures his patients but his way of being with them.' This is absolutely fundamental to the Laingian position.

Therapists would do well to follow the example of Socrates, the wisest of men according to the Oracle of Delphi. In the 'Apology' Socrates said, 'It seems to me that he is not referring literally to Socrates but has merely taken my name as an example, as he would say to us "The wisest of you men is he who has realised, like Socrates, that in respect of wisdom he is really worthless." '[10]

When Socrates learnt of the Oracle's judgement he embarked on a search to see whether it could be true. He went to learn from a politician who was purported to be wise. But Socrates realised, 'Well, I am certainly wiser than this man. It is only too likely that neither of us has any knowledge to boast of; but he thinks that he knows something which he does not know, whereas I am quite conscious of my ignorance. At any rate it seems that I am wiser than he is to this small extent, that I do not think I know what I do not know.'[11]

CHAPTER THREE

A Very Special State of Mind

> I mistrust all systemisers and avoid them. The will
> to a system is a lack of integrity.
>
> Nietzsche[1]

I once attended a lecture by William Gillespie – a long time President of the International Association of Psychoanalysis. During the course of his lecture he said that one could justifiably speak of a Laius complex – referring to the murderous hatred that Laius felt towards his son Oedipus. Anna Freud, who was in the audience, laughed heartily at the idea. I however had recently been thinking the same thing and had taken the trouble to look up some of the references to this notion in the analytic literature. So, after the lecture I went up to Gillespie and started to discuss the issue with him. At one point I mentioned that Freud had completely misrepresented the Oedipus play since Oedipus was the only character of any moral worth in his family. Though he killed his father it was in self-defence, and when his wife realised that Oedipus, her husband, was in fact her son, she tried to conceal the fact from him and to perpetuate the relationship. Whereas Oedipus would stop at nothing to uncover the truth, even though doing so involved his undoing. At this Gillespie refused to talk to me, turned his back and walked away. I was flabbergasted. Here, I'd imagined, must be a man who was interested in the truth and in discussing these matters honestly and openly – not a bit of it. The whole thing was a question of dogma – not open to discussion – what I was saying was blasphemy.

'We are strangers to one another, and their virtues are even more opposed to my taste than are their falsehoods and loaded dice.'[2] So wrote Nietzsche about scholars in *Thus Spake Zarathustra*. It is my sentiment about most psychoanalysts: 'When they give themselves out as wise their little sayings and truths make me shiver; their wisdom often smells as if it came from the swamp: and indeed, I have heard the frog croak in it!'[3]

Soshitsu Sen XV – the great Japanese Tea Master, in his book *Tea Life, Tea Mind* wrote: 'A Monk once asked his Master, "No matter what lies ahead, what is the Way?" The Master quickly replied, "The way is your daily life." '[4] This concept is at the very centre of the Way of Tea.

It is also at the very centre of the Way of Therapy – as Laing understood it. In an article by Paul Mezan on Laing in *R. D. Laing The Man and His Ideas* the following dialogue takes place – Laing is talking: 'But I really think most of the rules of analysis are more for the analyst's benefit than the patient's, for without those controls, he might freak out, not know who or where he was. But that's the risk if he wants to do psychoanalysis.'

'That puts a tremendous burden on the analyst', I commented. 'He has to be in a very special state of mind. That's how an analyst ought to be! That's what being an analyst is all about! And it shouldn't be a burden to him either. He should be doing that any time, effortlessly and completely willingly.'[5]

Perhaps the best account of this state of mind is to be found in Barbara Hannah's book, *Jung – His Life and Work*. She says that Jung advised her never to give a course of lectures without recounting the following experience of his great friend, Richard Wilhelm, a Sinologist and missionary in China.

'Richard Wilhelm was in a remote Chinese village which was suffering a most unusually prolonged drought. Everything had been done to put an end to it, and every kind of prayer and charm had been used, but all to no avail. So the elders of the village told Wilhelm that the only thing to do was to send for a rainmaker from a distance. This interested him enormously and he was careful to be present when the rainmaker arrived. He came in a covered cart, a small wizened old man. He got out of the cart, sniffed the air in distaste, then asked for a cottage on the outskirts of the village. He made the condition that no one should disturb him and that his food should be put down outside the door. Nothing was heard of him for three days, then everyone woke up to a downpour of rain. It even snowed, which was unknown at that time of year.

'Wilhelm was greatly impressed and sought out the rainmaker, who had now come out of his seclusion. Wilhelm asked him in wonder; "So you can make rain?" The old man scoffed at the very idea and said of course he could not. "But there was the most persistent drought until you came", Wilhelm retorted, "and then within three days – it rains?" "Oh" replied the old man, "that was something quite different. You see, I came from a region where everything is in order, it rains when it should and it is fine when that is needed, and the people here, they were all out of Tao and of themselves. I was at once infected when I arrived, so I had to be quite alone until I was once more in Tao and then naturally it rained." '[6]

Jung was so keen on this incident because it emphasised so well the message that it isn't what a therapist knows that brings about change but rather it is his state of Being in the world that heals.

I want to make it clear that what I feel, experience and know, is demanded of a psychotherapist in terms of his Being in the world, goes far beyond anything that a psychotherapy course provides.

Laing had said to Mezan that the analyst should be in the special state of mind any time. 'Any time?' Mezan asked. 'You mean not just in the office cemented behind the couch, but in real life too?' Maybe, I thought, we're getting to it, the thing about this man that people find so out of the ordinary. For the state of mind he is casually recommending is no everyday occurrence, no ordinary state of attentiveness picked up at your local psychiatric institute. People who are habitually in it have usually been called saints or buddhas, rarely psychoanalysts.'[7]

The issue that needs to be addressed is that the two most prominent psychotherapists in the world in the past forty years have both argued in this vein and yet the bias of training in psychotherapy is still almost universally towards the acquisition of knowledge and an identification with the medical model. So are Laing and Jung wrong or is everyone else? Perhaps it needs to be recognised that over a forty-year period only a few, perhaps only two, people may possess all of the qualities that are required to be able to meet the vast span of emotional, intellectual, physical and spiritual needs that those who go to them for help present them with. But we also need to worry that the conventional psychotherapy training may actually prevent someone transcending their less gifted teachers. My view is that such training prohibits the sort of individual growth and development in the trainees that they are being schooled to supposedly help others to develop.

One of the major figures in psychoanalysis was Melanie Klein. Klein trained Wilfred Bion who eventually became an eminent analyst himself. In his book on the clinical significance of the work of Bion the noted psychoanalyst, Donald Melzer, wrote of his early work that 'Bion was experiencing a sort of psychoanalytical latency period in which dutifulness was indeed dulling his creativity – and perhaps his critical judgement.

'In summary then a fairly unmistakable impression results from taking these two papers, the Review and Imaginary Twin, together; namely, that psycho-analytical training has had an oppressive effect upon Bion. It is perhaps one of the great limitations of this sort of training that the personal analysis takes so long to "recover from", to use a phrase Bion employed in his 1976 lecture at the Tavistock Centre. In this regard one should note that all Bion's major publications came after the death of Mrs Klein in 1960.'[8] It has been suggested that it takes at least seven years to recover from training as a psychoanalyst. No one has ever said how many never do so.

The possibility that only a few people may have the necessary qualities to really master psychotherapy is not as extreme as it might seem. As I have mentioned before, I originally trained to be a classical guitarist. When I was first interested in the guitar there were three major figures on the international scene – Andres Segovia, Julian Bream and John Williams. A phenomenal surge of interest in the guitar took place all over the world. In Japan alone there were two million classical guitar students in the seventies, and yet up to the time of Segovia's death a couple of years ago there were still only Segovia, Julian Bream and John Williams at the pinnacle of the guitar world. We look in vain today to find a painter of the stature of Picasso, though there are hundreds of thousands of painters; a sculptor of the standing of Henry Moore; or a philosopher as significant as Russell or Wittgenstein.

Let me illustrate the point further. With Laing out of the country, I didn't know who to recommend the girlfriend of a patient of mine to see for therapy. Then I remembered that a woman psychoanalyst had been recommended to me as being particularly successful at helping people who had suffered from a rejecting mother. The girlfriend went to see her. The analyst was horror-struck when when she learnt that sometimes I saw my patient socially, and warned the girlfriend to have nothing to do with me. She bragged that she was a totally different person outside the consultation room from in it, as if such a split in her behaviour – precisely the sort of problem people enter therapy to be cured of – was something to be proud of. After a few sessions the girlfriend asked her when she would start to have regular sessions to which the woman replied that she wasn't the sort of person who she would want to take on as a patient and that she was going to see her again and then pass her on to someone else. She complained that the girl didn't talk enough. Naturally the poor girl was shocked. She suddenly found herself in what is

most patients' worst fantasy. The analyst was totally oblivious of how destructive she was being. My patient's girlfriend
has since come to see me for therapy – is making excellent
progress and certainly has no difficulty in talking.

Compare this analyst's very paranoid response to hearing
that I had social contact with my patient, with Laing's deeply
moving account of his relationship with a fourteen-year-old
'psychotic' patient. It is taken from *Wisdom, Folly and Madness*.
'I thought that if he were consigned to a mental hospital aged
fourteen (there was no adolescent unit) however poor his
prognosis, this could only make it worse. Indeed, he could
probably be finished for life.

'He came to stay with us – my wife Anne and me and
three children under four.

'Everything went incredibly well from the start.'[9]

The humanity, loving concern and kindness that Laing
manifested here is in such contrast to the inhuman indifference
and sadism – disguised as professionalism – that the analyst
perpetrated.

A little later on Laing illustrates just how far this avoid-
ance of any normal, healthy interaction goes.[10]

'In a recent seminar that I gave to a group of psychoanalysts, my audience became progressively aghast when I
said that I might accept a cigarette from a patient without
making an interpretation. I might even offer a patient a
cigarette. I might even give him or her a light.

"And what if a patient asked you for a glass of water?"
one of them asked, almost breathlessly.

"I would give him or her a glass of water and sit down
in my chair again."

"Would you not make an interpretation?"

"Very probably not."

A lady exclaimed "I'm totally lost." '

In his postscript Laing says; 'Whatever else was going
on in psychiatry, it was, and is, one interface in the social-
economic-political structure of our society where camaraderie,
solidarity, companionship, communion is about impossible,

or completely impossible. Psychiatrists and patients were, or are, too often ranged on opposite sides. Before we meet, we are far apart.

'The psychiatrist-patient rift across the sane-mad line seemed to play a part in some of the misery and disorder occurring within the field of psychiatry. Maybe this loss of human camaraderie was the most important thing. Maybe it's restoration was the *sine qua non* of treatment.' This applies as much to psychotherapy as to psychiatry.

Laurens Van Der Post narrates the following beautiful account of Jung's treatment of a young peasant girl who everybody thought was going mad. 'A doctor in some remote valley in the mountain where she lived had heard of Jung and sent her to him. After talking to her for a while Jung realised that analysis would not do for her at all, and yet what else could he do? He watched the nice, plump, simple peasant girl, totally at a loss, and as he watched her, from far away in his past he heard his mother singing a cradle song. He immediately saw what the girl needed, took her on his lap, cradled her and hummed his mother's song to her – and at once he felt all the tension going out of her, and at the end of the song he seated her on the chair again and got her to tell him about her childhood. In the process they danced some nursery dances together and sang some songs together and played some children's games. At the end of the day he sent her to the mountains, and did not hear of her again until twenty-five years later at some medical conference. There he met the doctor who had sent the girl to him, and the doctor said to him, 'I have always wanted to ask you what you did to effect the miraculous cure on that unhappy girl I sent you.' Jung told me he was most embarrassed because he knew the conventional Swiss doctor would never understand if he told him. But he said, 'All I did was to sing my mother's cradle song, recite some nursery rhymes and listen to some stories, and that was all she needed to recover the honour with herself of which our kind of life had deprived her.' 'I hope this gives you' said Van Der Post, 'some understanding of

the enormous range and profound humanity of the man and
his love, his great objective love of our problematical nature.
For me, in this almost total extent to which he achieved a
condition of wholeness and objective love, he was one of the
great religious phenomenon of all time.'[11]

Van Der Post has got right to the heart of the matter.
Just as a patient of mine said that it was in those sessions in
which I was just being myself and not being a therapist that
she gained benefit, so too did this simple peasant girl regain
her Self because Jung had the courage to be himself rather
than trying to be a therapist.

To return to the analyst I referred to earlier with regard
to my patient's girlfriend – the very idea that under no
circumstances should one socialise with one's patients is so
paranoid and unnatural that it is bound to affect the patient
and his view of himself. Often I think it is a rationalisation
for therapists who had parents who wouldn't get close to
them to re-enact that with their patients. Barbara Hannah
tells how Jung 'did not agree with the Freudian analyst who
... avoided all social contact with their patients outside
analysis, and he began to feel the need for opportunities to
get to know his patients and their reactions in a setting nearer
to life than the consulting room and the analytic hour.'[12]
Really it would have been better if Hannah had simply said
that Jung felt the need to get to know his patients 'in a setting
nearer to life' and left it at that, rather than going on about
wanting to study their reactions. That smacks of a rationalisation of something that doesn't need to be justified. 'Therapist' and 'patient' – how awful and limiting these terms are.
Therapist and patient should feel free to get to know one
another because that is what human beings do. Of course,
on the other hand, the therapist should have no more reason
to feel obliged to get to know a patient socially than anyone
else he meets in life.

Bernard Leach quoted Hamada making the same crucial
point: 'Take, for instance, eating an apple. The primitive took
it right off the tree and ate it, skin, seeds and all. But today

we seem to think that peeling it looks better, and then we cut it up and stew it and make a jam of it and prepare it in all kinds of ways. In preparing the apple, quite often we commit many errors on the way. But in just taking it off the tree and eating the whole thing, there are no mistakes to be made.'[13]

Hamada developed the same point in a conversation with Susan Peterson: '... compare dwarf trees in the garden and trees on the hill. If it's a dwarf tree, when the weather gets a little bit bad you bring it in the house, if it gets dry you give it water. You train the branch for the tree or you make it grow in the way that you want, or lengthen the branches or not, as you want. A traditional potter' [psychotherapist] 'is like a dwarf tree. In the case of the tree you have to be careful what the weather, the condition damp or dry; the garden tree is only half a tree, the other half depends on the care you give it.' 'A tree in the mountains grows by itself. I should like to be such a tree. The traditional potter' [psychotherapist] 'is aware of himself today ... that is not good! Why is the mountain tree good? The roots are most hardy, the trunk is the finest, the leaves and the branches will grow well even if you leave them alone – you don't have to bend or trim them, they're O.K.'[14]

One August evening when I was still far too influenced by my previous training as a therapist and in particular over this issue of socialising with patients I went, after a group session, to the pub with Ronnie Laing. When we were there he asked me if I felt alright. I didn't and and told him so – and why – that I felt awkward being there with him. To which he replied 'Why can't we just be two people in a pub having a drink?'

A therapist must seek to be entirely natural – entirely unselfconscious of his being a therapist; to act in accord with his inner nature; to be able to respond spontaneously and appropriately to the needs of the moment. 'To those who long only for flowers fain would I show them the full-blown spring which abides in the toiling buds of snow covered hills.'[15]

This brings us back to my dream of the Key to the Unconscious which was to be found lying on top of plain earth. This dream emphasises that what is most priceless and sought after is to be found in what is most humble and natural.

In the Far East the value of this insight has long been appreciated. One of the most penetrating statements of this aesthetic is to be found in another essay by Soetsu Yanagi. The essay is about the Kizaeman tea bowl which is considered to be the finest in the world.

Yanagi had waited for a long time to see the bowl and you can imagine the sense of anticipation and excitement as it was slowly taken out of the fine boxes, one within another, in which it was contained.

'When I saw it my heart fell. A good tea bowl, yes, but ordinary! So simple, no more ordinary thing could be imagined. There is not a trace of ornament, not a trace of calculation. It is just a Korean food bowl, a bowl, more-over, that a poor man would use every day — commonest crockery.

'A typical thing for his use, costing next to nothing; made by a poor man; an article without the flavour of personality; used carelessly by its owner; bought without pride; something anyone could have bought anywhere and everywhere. That is the nature of this bowl. The clay had been dug from the hill at the back of the house; the glaze was made with the ash from the hearth; the potter's wheel had been irregular. The shape revealed no particular thought; it was one of many. The work had been fast; the turning was rough, done with dirty hands; the throwing slipshod; the glaze had run over the foot. The throwing room had been dark. The kiln was a wretched affair; the firing careless. Sand had stuck to the pot, but nobody minded; no one invested the thing with any dreams. It is enough to make one give up working as a potter.

'In Korea such work was left to the lowest. What they made was broken in kitchens, almost an expendable item.

The people who did this were clumsy yokels, the rice they ate was not white, their dishes were not washed. If you travel you can find these conditions anywhere in the Korean countryside. This, and no more, was the truth about this, the most celebrated Tea-bowl in the land. But that was as it should be. The plain and unagitated, the uncalculated, the harmless, the straightforward, the natural, the innocent, the humble, the modest; where does beauty lie if not in these qualities? The meek, the austere, the inornate – they are the natural characteristics that gain man's affection and respect. More than anything else, this pot is healthy, made for a purpose, made to do work. Sold to be used in everyday life. If it were fragile, it would not serve its purpose. By its very nature, it must be robust. Its healthiness is implicit in its function. Only a commonplace practicality can guarantee health in something made.

'One should correctly say, perhaps that there is no chance for it to fall sick, for it is a perfectly ordinary rice bowl used every day by the poor. It's not made with thought to display effects of details, so there is not time for the disease of technical elaboration to creep in. It's not inspired by theories of beauty, so there is no occasion for it to be poisoned by over-awareness. There is nothing in it to justify inscribing it with the maker's name. No optimistic ideals gave it birth, so it cannot become the plaything of sentimentality. It is not the product of nervous excitement, so it does not harbour the seeds of perversion. It was created with a very single purpose, so it shuns the world of brilliance and colour. Why should such a perfectly ordinary bowl be so beautiful! The beauty is an inevitable outcome of this ordinariness.

'Those who like the unusual are immune to the ordinary, and if they are aware of it at all, they regard it as a negative virtue. They conceive active beauty as our duty. Yet the truth is odd. No tea-bowl exceeds an Ido bowl in beauty. All beautiful Tea-bowls are those obedient to nature. Natural things are healthy things. There are many kinds of art, but none better than this. Nature produces more startling results than artifice. The most detailed human knowledge is puerile before the wisdom of nature. Why should beauty emerge from the world of the ordinary? The answer is ultimately because that world is natural.'[16]

The great Japanese potter, Shoji Hamada, wrote a short preface to the book. His writing is characteristically simple and unbelievably wise. Hamada wrote: 'In the Autumn of 1964 an international exhibition of contemporary studio pottery was held in Tokyo. Most of the work selected came from Europe, America, and Japan and was "abstract" in character, clearly showing the pressures of present day life and art.

'I felt a general lack of maturity both in motivation and technique. The first impression given was one of power, of force, but it was followed by a sensation of violence and at the same time of emptiness. On the whole, the Japanese exhibits had a greater traditional content and were more skilful in technique, but were less alive than the pots from the West. Shells without fish. The abstract examples were mannered and did not spring from a genuine internal life. In the whole exhibition, the pots I admired most were made by Bernard Leach. Many other Japanese potters agreed with me. Curiously, these were the quietest pots in the whole show. Whether he works in the East or the West he preserves a simple and straightforward approach. The focus of his work has been apparent for over fifty years. The feeling in his pots comes from a high inspiration that defeats both weakened tradition and the violence of modern motivation I have mentioned. He draws his strength from the soil of his own nature and his life experience. This is spring water. I feel the difference between this inspiration and that of others very strongly.'[17]

Every therapist should pay the greatest attention to these words.

In his book *Gandhi the Man*, Eknath Easwaran quotes Gandhi as saying 'There comes a time when an individual becomes irresistible and his action becomes all-pervasive in its effect. This comes when he reduces himself to zero.'[18]

Psychotherapists, particularly psychoanalysts, are generally as far removed from these attitudes as is possible to
imagine. I say psychoanalysts in particular because there is
so much pressure upon analysts to produce papers and write
books in order to get ahead.

Part of the problem stems from the fact that therapists
conduct their work in private. Therefore, the only way to
become well known quickly is to produce an original idea
and publish it. This places far too much emphasis on doing
rather than being and takes the individual completely away
from the attitude that is needed for continued growth in
therapist and patient.

Compare this with Hamada and what he had to say to
his friend Kawai, when he, Hamada, had returned from
England after spending several years in St Ives with Leach.
'When I came back from England and he asked me immediately what kind of work I planned to do in the future, I
realised he had been stripped clean of all the courage he had
originally. I said I was not interested in making or creating
something novel or refined or acceptable from the standpoint
of the usual idea of beauty, but that I was aiming at making
correct and healthy things, pottery that's practical and not
forced, that responds to the nature of the materials. I did not
want to make something outwardly beautiful, but to begin
from the inside; health and correctness were more important
to me.'[19]

The attitudes required to develop a career within the
analytic fraternity are opposed to arriving at what I regard
as the right approach for a therapist to adopt towards his
career and himself, particularly because it leads towards super-
ficiality.

Later Leach quotes Hamada discussing the same issue
from a slightly different perspective: 'If one wishes to describe
Kawai in terms of water, below a waterfall there is a deep
pool; the depths of the pool are unmoving and silent. But
Kawai is the water that spills out of this pool and splashes
and sprays noisily into shallower places. In Japanese this is

called sessaragi. The deep pool, the soundless water represents potential energy. The deeper the water, of course, the more silent it is. This is not for Kawai. He is not satisfied with this. He prefers the movements and dynamics of the splashing water; he likes to see the movement and have the movement be seen.'[20]

And he quotes Yanagi writing this on Hamada: 'It is Hamada's endeavour to draw as close as he can to the world that is natural, common and single. Some may regard this pottery as crude and coarse, yet it has been made only after the most careful consideration and thought. Nearly all potters of today are walking precariously like acrobats on a tightrope in their desire to do something extraordinary, whereas Hamada only wishes to make plain the truth that the most healthy and natural beauty comes from simplicity. No modern potter seems ever to have thought, much less to have done, what he is doing. For to build up solidly on these simple foundations is an almost impossible undertaking for the sophisticated individualistic potter of today, who's desirous of distinguishing himself by doing something unusual. Those who are without wisdom and will cannot hope to stand firm against the many temptations that surround them; for in the long run the problem of beauty is the problem of conscience.'[21]

This applies just as much to psychotherapists. It really lies at the very hub of the difficulties where psychotherapy is concerned. If one follows Jung's advice that I quoted in an earlier chapter and does not apply any theory to one's patients, then there is very little to be written about psychotherapy. Now, as most people are aware, a major publishing industry has built up around it — almost all of which, to be frank, isn't worth the paper it's written on. It is absurd too, that the status of a therapist should be determined by his capacity to write. I can think of no other profession where a person's value is judged on the basis of their ability to do something other than the service that people go to them for.

In order to produce papers that will get their name known,

analysts have to abstract tiny aspects of a few individuals' behaviour in order to have something to write about. But breaking people down into bits, as Laing has frequently and eloquently argued, is an activity that takes the analysts further away from the people that he is trying to understand – and further away from the healthy mental attitude that allows the therapist to have the deepest insight and to be of the greatest benefit to those who come to him.

The dangers are even greater now as television dominates people's experience of life. The worry here is that too much emphasis will come to be placed upon personality as a means of evaluating the relative merit of therapists.

As Hamada said (and it applies as much to therapists):- 'People who are making things must put out an antenna above everyone else's head and a probe in the earth deeper than anyone. Having what you call an individual character isn't very useful; just words, no good.' And later, 'You must have done a very great deal before you are worthy to speak about it.'

Unfortunately there are enormous pressures upon people to be successful at a young age and this again makes the more ambitious therapist more concerned with doing than being. The main aim can easily become to produce something that is original.

'Ordinary people' said Hamada in the same conversation, 'think that "good" is too difficult a concept, so people are content thinking that if it is different it is good. They are fooled by that and like to make things that are shocking or will surprise people and they fool the public. Within what is fashionable at the time they try to make something that is different and within the fashion at the time they look for a hole and try to pull something through it, something for their vanity, or to show themselves off. That's the usual reason for making. The ordinary person who thinks he is creating something is doing this instead. Shiko Munakata says, "I am not responsible for my work". That's very interesting. He sells his woodblocks at a high price and has always had a famous reputation, but still he says that we don't bear a responsibility for that. This attitude of not bearing responsibility is the true attitude of bearing responsibility.'

The essence of the right attitude to being a therapist is that the therapist learns to let his unconscious do all of the work. He becomes a vessel for the unconscious. The more he can say what comes into his mind without censoring it, the more valuable the help that he gives his patients will be.

Thus, to return to my nescience dream – the state of not knowing is the true state of knowing. It is rare to find a therapist who can be honest about this.

At the very end of his life, Jung expressed this in very beautiful terms in his autobiography:- 'When people say I am wise, or a sage, I cannot accept it. A man once dipped a hatful of water from a stream. What did that amount to? I am not that stream. I am at the stream, but I do nothing. Other people are at the same stream, but most of them find they have to do something with it. I do nothing. I never think that I am the one who must see to it that cherries grow on stalks. I stand and behold, admiring what nature can do.

'There is a fine story about a student who came to a rabbi and said, "In the olden days there were men who saw the face of God. Why don't they any more?" The rabbi replied, "Because nowadays no one can stoop so low."

'One must stoop a little in order to fetch water from the stream.'[22]

In the last paragraph of the book Jung wrote, 'When Lao-Tzu says: "All are clear, I alone am clouded," he is expressing what I now feel in advanced old age.'[23] But how many books can you write saying that! And how many people will realise that someone who can say that is more knowledgeable than someone who is stuffed full of theories. As Jung once said, 'Thank God I am Jung and not a Jungian.'

CHAPTER FOUR

Difficulties Along the Way

> I think if you think along the lines of nature then you think properly
>
> C. G. Jung

A few years ago I was delighted to come across *C. G. Jung and Herman Hesse — A Record of Two Friendships* by Miguel Serrano, a Chilean writer, explorer and diplomat. When on the first page I read, 'Even today, I would go halfway round the world to find a book if I thought it essential to my needs.... I would go without eating in order to get a book, and I have never liked borrowing books, because I have always wanted them to be absolutely mine, so that I could live with them for hours on end'[1] I knew that I had found a man after my own heart. Serrano's book has an extraordinary lyrical quality about it — a poetic luminosity that is a reflection of his profoundly sensitive nature.

Towards the end of the work Serrano quotes himself talking to Jung: 'Years ago I had an experience I want to tell you about', I said. 'When I was a very young boy, I used to have the feeling at night, that I was dividing, or splitting away from myself. These feelings were always preceded by vibrations which rose along the length of my body, starting from the soles of my feet. These vibrations varied in intensity, but in the end they grew so powerful that I was afraid I was going to die. I remember one in particular when the vibrations became virtually unendurable; and then suddenly, right in front of me, a basin appeared. As though commanded to do so, I thrust my hands into into the basin and then spread the strange liquid it contained all over my body. Immediately the vibration ceased. All this took place in a state which was by no means dreamlike; it was entirely real – indeed, on a plane of reality far higher than that of ordinary perception. But I was never able to retain that degree of reality when, so to speak, I returned to my own body and found myself lying in bed. For years I tried to produce those same phenomena voluntarily.'[2]

Dr Jung then made this observation; 'As I said, those are all subjective experiences, they are not collectively verifiable. What you call vibrations may only have been dreams, or at most, manifestations of the Collective Unconscious.'

Serrano continued, 'I was disappointed by Jung's answer. He seemed incapable of penetrating these mysteries, and for a sad moment, I had the feeling that all he had done in his work was to create a new terminology to explain old truths. I had been similarly disappointed by the Dalai Lama, who had made no revealing statements about my phenomena, but had relied on ancient dogma. He had been afraid of exceeding himself as the head of a church, and in the presence of his court officials. It is always a heavy task to be responsible for a body of organised religious doctrine – or for a school of scientific psychology. I then realised that I would never find any guidance, or explanation, for my personal experience' – which for Jung, were purely subjective – 'I knew that I would have to rely solely upon my own intuition. I would have to walk alone, as Jung himself had once done, along the "razors edge"' Serrano gets right to the heart of the matter where Jung's response was concerned.

Having read this I really found myself in a dilemma because I am very loathe to impose my interpretations upon someone who hasn't asked for them, although here I felt that Miguel Serrano was in effect asking for answers but had given up hope of anyone providing them. On the other hand I felt strongly that I knew exactly what his experience was about. But then this too created difficulties, because the nature of what I had to say was so unusual and potentially shocking that I was not only concerned that he would reject it out of hand, but was equally worried about how he would be affected if he accepted it.

I did eventually write to him. The main point I made was that I believed that the vividness and intensity of Miguel's experience was due to it being a memory rather than a fantasy. I told him that I believed that the experience being relived was his birth. The vibrations seemed to me to relate to uterine contractions. What came across very strongly was that he had come very close to death at this time. I made other comments too, but no longer remember what they were.

I didn't get a reply, which surprised me, as I was sure that Miguel Serrano would have written to me if only to say that he disagreed. Then quite out of the blue, some months later I received this letter;

Dear Anthony Lunt,

It is phantastic! After more than three months your letter arrived here in Chile where I am living now after ten years in the Swiss Ticino, in the old house of Herman Hesse. You wrote your letter the 12 September, two days after my birthday. I am Virgo and something to do with water and the Virgin (virginal conception) of course.

As always your letter arrived in the right moment producing a tremendous trial I must deal with it.

First in my book I didn't explain chronologically my experience to Professor Jung and that can lead to some wrong conclusions. The splitting or the dividing of myself it was almost a childhood experience, at fourteen maybe sixteen years old or so. But the vibration was a much later phenomena. Some time before my initiation. It was this experience which 'synchronistically' pushed me towards the encounter with my Master and consequently initiation by him. It was after this initiation that, trying to produce myself consciously and by will the vibrations, that I came near the boundaries of death. Then the basin with water appeared in front of me and saved me. You are right, a phantastic blissful state developed from it.

Reading your letter suddenly came to my memory the following recollection: When I was a child somebody showed me a big crystal jug and told me that with that jug they brought me to life because I was born asphyxiated. In order that I could breath they dropped on me the full jug of cold water. Is it not extraordinary?

My mother died when I was five or six years old. She was twenty-three. My father died when I was eight years old. He was thirty-three. Like Parzival I was a wild orphan and I grew up as a 'pure man in the wild forest' of the south polar regions. Since then I am searching for the Grail which is a jug, but although it is a stone, a lapsit exilis.

I will agree with your deep and essential explanation but since I think that I understand you and I feel that you are not of this kind of psychologist who have the mania to reduce everything high to low, I would be delighted to play with you the Bach concerto for two violins. That means as two warriors or two searchers trying to complete one to each other by the way of vivencial experience....

I was, and am, very impressed by Miguel Serrano's open-mindedness and willingness to face the horrifying issues involved. His account shows how affected one can be by very early experiences, and it shows how these strange happenings can be given meaning in precisely the same way that dreams can be – with the same beneficial results.

The following horrifying account involves a patient of mine. Michael, a pale gaunt utterly hopeless figure, sat before me in the consultation room with a look of such misery in his eyes that I found it almost unbearable to look at him. He began to tell me that he hadn't worked for nine years and that this was due to his experiencing the most appalling panic attacks.

The first attack took place when he was camping with two friends in a field. One of them had forgotten something while they were going for a walk. Michael offered to fetch it. He ran to the tent, retrieved the article and turned, looking back at his friends as he did so. At this moment he was overwhelmed by a dreadful attack of panic that struck like lightning from nowhere. He felt appallingly ill and was unable to function. The next attack took place when he was with a friend walking along the road. The final blow came when he was walking to work alone. On this occasion he was so convinced that he was going to die that he returned home and was not able to work again. Whenever Michael experienced these attacks he was sure that his heart was going to stop and that he was dying. The dread of experiencing such total panic imprisoned him within a tiny radius of his home. For years he had been unable to travel in a car on a motorway. If he was too far away from home he felt so unbearably ill that it wasn't worth making the effort to go anywhere. Medical treatment had proved to be totally ineffective.

The more Michael talked the more it seemed to me that what he was describing was a catastrophic memory of something that had actually happened early in his life. When I asked him about his birth he said that he had been a twin and that the other baby had been stillborn. I then felt sure that what he suffered from was a memory of his birth. He decided to ask his mother what his birth had been like.

He arrived at the next session already looking better and then excitedly told me of the following account that he had received from his mother. She told him for the first time that he had actually been one of triplets but the third child had died a few months after conception (looking back at his two friends). For a while things went well but tragically the other child, a brother, died before the pregnancy had gone full term (the panic as he walked to work with his friend). And then when birth actually did take place, Michael's heart stopped – he too died – but was revived (the panic when journeying on his own). Michael now had a context in which his terror of death made sense. The fear of motorways had the same origin. What paralysed him was the fact that, as in birth, once committed to the motorway he couldn't stop.

But there was a further grisly twist to his life. Matters had come to a head the summer before when his best friend hanged himself from the banisters. He had unconsciously chosen a friend with whom he was very close to re-enact the awful trauma of the loss of his brother and of being trapped in the womb with the corpse of his dead brother squashed against him. As time passed and we looked at these issues, Michael was at last able to function again to the point where he was able to get a job as a driving instructor.

The worst symptoms are often memories. The experiences they embody are usually so horrible or so far back that the person re-enacts them rather than remember them and this applies particularly to death. Again it is a question of giving meaning to these symptoms. A medical analysis is useless. It is equivalent to analysing the constituents of the canvas on which Rembrandt had painted and of analysing the oil and the paint without paying any attention to the portrait itself. Many physical 'illnesses' come into this category. Not all have to do with pre-birth events of course. It would be absurd to apply any such formula.

Maureen hasn't long been seeing me. She is an attractive, very intelligent, woman in her thirties. One of her many problems is a preoccupation with death − thinking about herself as dead both in her dreams and her day dreams. For instance she dreamed that she was laid out on a bed of flowers and smiling contentedly as people came to look at her. Coupled with this there has been a compulsive need to spend long periods of time − sometimes all day, just lying down and staring up at the ceiling.

Maureen had no idea where the preoccupation with being dead came from. She became aware of her spending so long flat on her back as she gave more attention to the issues springing from her earliest childhood. It quickly became apparent that although Maureen is able to hold down a very well paid responsible job effectively, once she is alone in her house she slips back into the way of life of an infant and when she is more disturbed − of a foetus. For instance she would sometimes spend hours sitting by the telephone (which is itself shaped like a foetus connected via the cord/umbilicus to the outside world). She was trapped inside the house as if she were enclosed within a womb. The kitchen in particular represented the womb to her. She felt strangely anxious about it − longed to be fed without her having to cook or even eat food (through the umbilicus). She generally just cooked mashed potato − which was the nearest adult equivalent to baby food that she could tolerate. Once into the treatment she developed a passion for using a baby's bottle. It became apparent from the way in which she was so negligent in her treatment of herself that she had been very poorly cared for as a baby. Her mother was a very disturbed woman who was herself very infantile. I suggested therefore that perhaps the lying down for hours on end re-enacted her mother leaving her in a pram for very extended periods of time. Her father confirmed that this was so and this symptom rapidly lost its appeal for her.

At about the same time she had to babysit for her grandmother − yet another very disturbed, infantile adult − who lived with Maureen's mother and who had totally dominated the family. Maureen took advantage of this opportunity to question her grandmother about her own life − something she had never done before. In doing so she unexpectedly learnt the explanation of her preoccupation with being dead. Her grandmother told her that her own mother had died when she was born. She was then fostered out to a family but was eventually taken away by her father when she was seven. The foster mother was so shattered by this that she died shortly after. So both of her grandmothers' mothers were associated with death. Maureen came to see how her grandmother, who continued to be a child, had brought up her own daughter − Maureen's mother − to mother her. But this meant that she had to be a dead mother. Then Maureen's mother brought up Maureen, who had, like her, never really had a mother herself – since the grandmother had only been brought up to be a daughter – to be this ideal but dead great grandmother. And since her grandmother had only known her own mother when she was in the womb – they all lived an intra-uterine existence. She later learnt that her other great grandmother died giving birth too!

It is by no means rare for people to be living the life of an ancestor. One woman, for instance, came to me having had a very long-standing affair with a leading figure in the town. She was in a terrible state because for years she had tried to decide whether she wanted to be with him or with her very ordinary but loving husband. After some weeks of therapy she suddenly realised that her mother had done exactly the same thing and not only that but her grandmother, who was a servant, had a very longstanding affair with the Lord of the Manor. My patient realised that she had been repeating a pattern that had been laid down by her grand-mother. She was re-enacting her grandmother's affair and so really had to choose between her grandmother's life or her own. She chose to be herself, to give up the glamour of the affair and to stay with her husband.

I can't stress enough what should now be obvious – that it is simply impossible to use any theory to arrive at the solutions to problems such as these.

A very ambitious young man came to see me having been recommended by another patient of mine. He had an air of desperate confidence about him. A curious mixture. He told me that his ambition was to be able to retire at thirty-nine. But a major obstacle in his life was that he was invariably sick in any social situation and often at other times too. Eventually it became apparent that his sickness was an identi-fication with his mother's vomiting when she suffered from terminal cancer. She had died when she was forty. What my patient had done was to identify with his mother. His ambition to retire at thirty-nine was a desperate denial of the identification and at the same time an expression of it. Like her, he would stay working until he was thirty-nine – but he was trying to make out that this was his choice whereas she had had none. Behind this was the idea that he too would be dead at forty and hence unable to work. His vomiting disappeared and his ambition reduced to more manageable proportions.

Sometimes I can only stare in horrified amazement at the implications of some symptoms. A man in his forties came to see me having been unable to work for several months. Despite extensive medical examinations no medical condition could be diagnosed. None the less he was so weak that he was completely unable to work and suffered from very disturbing symptoms such as acute dizziness and unsteadiness on his feet. It was on the afternoon of 5 November that he suddenly, for no explicable reason, experienced his first attack of terrible dizziness and felt unable to stand up. We were never really able to explain why the 'attack' occurred at that time. Until last year when in the afternoon of 5 November his son inexplicably came off his motorbike a short distance from home and was killed. Some months before my patient became terrified of driving a car and this too seems to be related to foreknowledge of his son's death on the road.

Near miscarriages and abortion attempts can also be acted out. These are far more common than is usually imagined. The medical profession have taken the view that the baby is incapable of registering these experiences because the child's nervous system is incomplete until it is a year old. They use a mechanistic model treating the baby as if he is a mechanism, say a piece of electrical equipment – if all the parts aren't there it won't work. However the fact is that there is an enormous body of evidence to prove that people can and do remember their earliest experiences. Much of this is dealt with in the analytic literature, as in Laing's *Facts of Life* and *The Voice of Experience*. For the purposes of this book I think I can best make my point by giving an example of my own experience. It was this incident that impressed upon me that even the earliest events of our lives are recalled and this has made it clear to me that in some way memory is completely separate from the nervous system and that it is far more in keeping with many people's experience in therapy. That in some way there is a capacity for memory in the single cell, and these memories can be re-enacted with one's own children.

One Thursday evening I suddenly felt an intense desire to drink some gin. It wasn't too long before I was well and truly drunk. At that time I didn't have a girlfriend. I suddenly felt I had to have sex that night, so I went off to a local pick-up joint but was then so drunk that I made a complete fool of myself and staggered home. The next morning I didn't feel too bad. But as the morning progressed I felt unbelievably dreadful — far worse than I have ever felt from simply drinking too much. What was even more unbearable was the mental suffering that I began to go through. On three occasions I felt so desperately ill that I really thought I was going to die. As morning passed into afternoon things got no better, until suddenly at four in the afternoon the whole thing lifted. I spent some time wondering what on earth could have happened. Then it came to me that this was my conception date. I was born on 20 May and this was Friday 17 August.

When I asked my mother what happened at the time of my conception she said that she remembered it particularly well because the experience had been so unbearably awful. So for the first time she told me what had occurred. One Thursday night my parents had drunk some gin. They were particularly keen to conceive a child and so had intercourse that night. The next morning my mother had arranged to meet my father in London (they lived in Lewisham). As the morning progressed she felt more and more sick. She felt so ill that she had had to get off the bus three times. At these times she was convinced that she was dying. Nothing improved until at four o'clock she suddenly felt better. I had repeated almost exactly my mother's experience when I was conceived — which was of course my experience too since I was in her body.

Sometimes such experiences are recalled; sometimes, as in my case, they are acted out, and sometimes they are dreamed of. The better the therapist the more intuitive he is. But that doesn't mean haphazard or unpredictable in an unhealthy way. On the contrary there is a constancy that stems from intuition because it emerges from the very ground of one's being. The Self which is pure nature.

In practice we are talking about the therapist being able to trust and to utilise his psychic facilities during the treatment. Sometimes progress can only be made when the therapist is able to do this. For instance, at one time I had a particularly sensitive patient who was very psychic. For a few weeks she was virtually unable to talk during the sessions. So what I did was ask her a question and then wait to get the answer. It was by psychic means that I was able to pick up that her mother had been in an orphanage. This was subsequently verified. Unfortunately at that time I was very opposed to psychic issues. I accounted for what took place in the session in other terms, and I attacked the patient when she raised such questions. This is something that I regret very deeply. Of course I was able to justify it in terms of my conducting the treatment in a proper manner. This patient later said that she got no benefit at all from the sessions in which I was being a therapist. She only grew when I was being myself. And that really is the very heart of the matter.

It is well established that there is a period after a child is born, and probably before it, when there is an intense telepathic bond between mother and child. I have found that some of the people who come to me – often the most gifted and sensitive, certainly with the greatest potential – can only really become themselves if we can share and experience that psychic bond. I have several patients who I know are going to contact me if I've woken up thinking of them in the morning.

Often the patient acts in accordance with the impulse from the Self and feels himself to be in the position that Gandhi wrote of: 'And even if I have to face the prospect of a minority of one, I humbly believe I have the courage to be in such a hopeless minority. That to me is the only truthful position.' What is essential to growth is that the patient actually lives out – embodies – what he feels to be his being true to himself. Insight is not enough – one has to change one's behaviour in accordance with it.

The more the patient actualizes his inner life, the more he is able to differentiate between what is genuinely springing from his inner life and what has been accepted from, and often dumped on him by, others.

A lot of time in therapy is spent helping my patients to become aware of the gulf between what they do and what they want to do. Then having realised what they want to do, they have to understand the difficulties that come in the way of their putting these things into practice. I certainly feel that the intense meaning that life has for me is a result of my constantly striving to actualise my inner life. Living my life from inside out.

Now a lot of people will say that that sounds very selfish. On the contrary. If you conduct your life on that basis you become increasingly sensitive to the effect that you have upon others.

It is difficult to convince people who live life from the outside in, that doing the opposite is not being selfish. They feel deeply threatened, because living life from the inside out necessarily leads to change. Whereas those who live it from the outside in want life to be fixed.

Precisely the same danger applies to therapists who adhere too rigidly to a theoretical approach. As Alfred Reynolds wrote 'A final pitfall facing the absolute believer is that once truth is complete, generally valid and self evident for all time, he would claim, there remains no room for doubt and inquiry. Without the creative tension between the known and the unknown, the problem and man's inquisitive search for its solution, truth would die or degenerate into barren doctrine.... Those who HAVE the truth are therefore enemies of truth: to them any further quest appears as trespassing by the human intelligence upon sacred grounds. It is this attitude, more than their intolerance and untruthfulness, which turns the defenders of absolute truth into the foes of truth. Nietzsche puts it succinctly: "Be without jealousy of the Absolute, these urgent ones, O lover of truth. Never yet did truth consort with the absolute mind" (*Thus spake Zarathustra*).'[3]

Here Reynolds means personal truth when he speaks of truth. It is worth quoting what he has to say about it; 'Another approach to truth we may call (personal), in that it is unconditionally valid to its holder, and not necessarily to anyone else. It cannot claim general validity and certainly not finality. Its roots are in our personal experience (in all the aspects of our experience) and as it cannot be verified, it can only be demonstrated through our own lives. Since other people's experience differs from our own, their personal truths will, necessarily, differ from ours. We shall not merely suffer, but expect and welcome this difference, since the manifoldness of truth is the best evidence of its personal nature. For this reason, unconditional tolerance is a concomitant of personal truth.'[4]

' "Let us understand that accepted views are not digested truths!" They have little relevance in that they have no share in growth and no part in his attitude. "Knowledge cannot be acquired through opinion, or by taking it on the authority of others" says the great Islamic sage Al-Shafi. Any truth which is not transformed into "being" falls by the wayside, even if millions of men and women pay lip-service to it. On the other hand, if a truth is upheld and lived by a small number of people that truth "Lives".'[5]

'Personal truth grows through experience and understanding, by proceeding from choice to commitment. However, it can never reach finality. Doubt and inquiry too do not undermine but strengthen it. A ready-made doctrine may be endangered by doubt, but not the living growth of experienced and comprehended truth.'[6]

If one accepts this viewpoint, as I do, then it is clear that the therapist who helps many different types of people to face and resolve their difficulties must be open, sympathetic and responsive to the enormous diversity of human need and experience that they will present him with. I have tried to show earlier how Eastern thought is particularly sensitive to deep psychological issues and their practicalities. In this respect, too, they are often more aware of these needs than the traditional psychoanalyst.

Lam Thubten Yoshe wrote; 'A major characteristic of all Buddha's teachings is that they are designed to fit the needs and aptitudes of each individual. Since we all have different interests, problems and ways of life, no one method of instruction could ever be suitable for everyone.... Thus there could be certain times when it might be necessary to say "yes" and others when it would be more appropriate to say "no", even in response to the same question.'[7]

The task that patient and therapist are faced with is how to have a relationship that will allow the patient to discover what it is to be truly himself. In Tibet the spiritual Gurus are sometimes also known as spiritual friends. This captures the essence of what the attitude of the therapist should be. The Greek word from which the term 'therapist' is derived means, as Laing has pointed out, an attendant. The function of the therapist is to attend in a caring and respectful way.

Laing captures this well in his very important paper *The Psychotherapeutic Experience* – in *The Politics of Experience*. Here Laing insisted that: 'Psychotherapy must remain an obstinate attempt of two people to recover the wholeness of being human through the relationship between them. Any technique concerned with the other without the self, with behaviour to the exclusion of experience, with the relationship to the neglect of the persons in relation, with the individuals to the exclusion of their relationship, and most of all, with an object-to-be-changed rather than a person-to-be-accepted, simply perpetuates the disease it purports to cure.'[8]

Laing continues a little later: 'The psychotherapeutic relationship is therefore a research. A search, constantly re-asserted and reconstituted for what we have all lost, and which some can perhaps endure a little more easily than others, as some people can stand lack of oxygen better than others, and this re-search is validated by the shared experience regained in and through the therapeutic relationship in the here and now.'[9]

CHAPTER FIVE

Keep One Foot in the Grave

> Your only obligation in any lifetime is to be true to yourself.[1]
>
> Richard Bach

But learning to be true to yourself is not easy. Opposition arises from three sources: the therapist, the patient and from those associated with the patient. Opposition from the therapist occurs if he acts out his own problems with the patient or is too conditioned by his training to be able to acknowledge and confirm the validity of aspects of the patient's experience or being. Laing points out this danger in *Self and Others*.

'Confronted with this woman's experience, clinical psychiatric terminology, in both its descriptive and theoretical aspects, is almost completely inadequate. Unless one can describe, one cannot explain.

One glimpses here the naked, intricate actuality of the complexity of experiences that those of us who do not deny what we cannot explain or even describe are struggling to understand. Theory can only legitimately be made on behalf of experience, not in order to deny experience which the theory ignores out of embarrassment.'[2]

One of Freud's most valuable empirical observations was of what he called the *'compulsion to repeat'*. We all tend to repeat the experiences that we have gone through in the past – particularly from our childhood. If these experiences were healthy and good then our lives will involve the repetition of these experiences and everything will be fine. But if they were unhappy then the individual will constantly tend to repeat unhappy situations. Thus a woman whose father was an alcoholic will be likely to marry an alcoholic herself. The French obstetrician, Frederic Leboyer, has argued that obstetricians repeat their own birth by imposing it upon their patients.

One reason why it is important for prospective psychotherapists to have therapy themselves is to resolve these childhood traumas so that they will be less likely to act them out with their patients.

In *Fundamental Questions of Psychotherapy* Jung wrote: 'The intelligent psychotherapist has known for years that any complicated treatment is an individual, dialectical process, in which the doctor, as a person, participates just as much as the patient. In any such discussion the question of whether the doctor has as much insight into his own psychic processes as he expects from his patient naturally counts for a very great deal, particularly in regard to the "rapport", or relationship of mutual confidence, on which the therapeutic success depends. The patient, that is to say, can win his own relationship to the doctor as a human being. ... We could say, without too much exaggeration, that a good half of every treatment that probes at all deeply consists in the doctors examining himself, for only what he can put right in himself, can he hope to put right in the patient.'[3]

He also made the following very important observation in a previous paragraph, that the therapist 'should remember that the patient is there to be treated and not to verify a theory'.

The same problem applies to the family and friends of a patient. We all tend to choose friends who confirm our view of the world and this relates to the choice of marital partner too, of course. Families can be enormously complex systems of collusion. As the patient gains insight into himself and others, he will often start to alter the assumptions that he has made about himself or to be unprepared to accept false attributions that are applied to him by others. His behaviour will hopefully change for the better but precisely this may be what is regarded as unacceptable. One patient of mine, who had been very disturbed, rapidly made progress during her treatment. Her family were alarmed by these changes and gathered to persuade her to go into a mental hospital. She was astonished and amused when it was said that the fact that she talked a lot now whereas before she said nothing was seen as convincing proof of her needing to be hospitalised. What should have been a cause for joy was turned into a means of persecution.

Many people encounter really fierce opposition to their changing and realise that those that profess to care for them would prefer them to suffer than to be free of the disturbance that they too are trapped by. The patient may threaten the assumptions that he and they have made about life, for instance that you should put up with a bad marriage or a bad job or that it is superior to be homosexual. Many patients find themselves shedding or being rejected by their friends and sometimes by their family too. This can be one of the most distressing consequences of treatment, particularly because it highlights the extent to which these others are only interested in the patient if he is as they want him to be. This is a very complicated issue that really deserves a book to itself.

Patients usually find that they have the attitude to themselves that their parents had towards them. A child whose parents ignored any of his achievements will have the same attitude towards any success he has in later life. This is an empirical, not a theoretical, statement. In itself it has no therapeutic value because it is the specifics of each individual's life that have to be related to, not the broad application of a general principal. Case histories too can create the illusion that one can gain real benefit from identifying with someone else's experience rather than exploring your own. None the less they make the discussion of these concerns a far more human undertaking. The following example illustrates in a particularly striking way how Jeremy, a middle-aged man who divorced his wife, managed to repeat earlier experiences and his parents' attitude towards him in such a destructive combination that it almost totally destroyed him.

From the start Jeremy's parents wanted a girl. His mother continued to see him as a girl after he was born. This was his first experience of his parents complete failure to be interested in who he actually was and their only seeing him as embodying the image that they had of him. The extent to which he, as an individual, completely failed to matter to them is illustrated by their forgetting about him and leaving him outside in a pram during an air raid while they hid in the shelter. When he first came to see me he had the manner and sickly charisma of a struggling, dandified, West End hairdresser.

His mother was a self-obsessed, hard, unfeeling woman and when he eventually found a replica of her, he married the girl. From the night of their wedding she made it clear that she wasn't interested in him and very shortly afterwards said she didn't love him. After a year or so of therapy he divorced her and then went through a period of isolation. Eventually he managed to meet someone who was even more unloving and destructive than his ex-wife and mother had been, and he started to pursue the relationship. It was immediately apparent to me that he was on a course to disaster and I strongly advised him to stop seeing her.

He paid as much attention to me as his parents had to him. He was totally convinced that he knew better than I and that I had some unsavoury motives for advising him as I did. I respected his right to do whatever he wanted with his life but continued to give firm expression to my perception of what was going on.

Jeremy kept a record of his dreams and of the events associated with them. As time passed he came to feel that what the dreams meant to him at the time that he dreamt them was a result of his seeing what he wanted to see in them, and that he completely failed to relate to the imagery that was actually presented in the dream. In relating to his inner life in this way he was repeating exactly his parents' responses to him both as a child and as an adult.

Jeremy went to a party with his new love, M., in July. At that point he had had no physical contact with her. The following week he gave her a kiss after which he had this dream: 'I was playing some sort of game where my mother was Hitler. She came at me with a knife. I caught hold of it in my hand, then she stabbed my bottom. I walked along with the knife still protruding.'

At the time Jeremy interpreted this dream as meaning that his mother inside him was furious about his kissing a woman and that she wanted to destroy him and for him to be homosexual. Subsequently he felt that M. manifested many of his mother's worst characteristics, that M. was Hitler and that she wanted to destroy him as she wanted to destroy all men. It seemed clear to him later that the dream was depicting how dangerous M. was.

He went to bed with her a few days later but was unable to have intercourse with her due to impotence (the healthiest response he could have had to the woman). This was followed by a dream: 'I was in bed with M. My ex-wife was outside the door but she came and kicked me in the balls. M. tried to protect me.'

Again he felt that this dream was depicting his internalised ex-wife, furious at his involvement with another woman. The dream convinced him of how caring M. was. Later he saw his ex-wife as representing all that was worst in M., whom he had split into a good and bad figure – relating only to the idealised and denying the negative.

This use of denial occurs in a dream of 3 August. 'I was trying to blow up a boat which was threatening me by using a box of matches.'

Jeremy saw this as depicting his ability to withstand attack – he was so able that he could blow up a large boat with a box of matches. Later he felt that the dream depicted the extent to which he was denying how serious the situation was becoming and how negligible was his ability to oppose it.

A few days later he dreamed; 'I was turning right into a

small road when two cars crashed behind me'.

I found these dreams alarming – even his dreams were denying that he was being damaged by the relationship. Other people's cars were crashing, not his. He was now becoming increasingly manic, devious and triumphant.

Two days later, after managing to make love to M., she became incredibly hostile saying that he was not strong or intelligent enough for her and demanding that he challenge her. He dreamed: 'An old man was lying in bed but only the top half of the man existed.' I felt that this dream accurately portrayed the state he was now in.

He increased his denial of the reality of his situation by not remembering any dreams for ten days – always a bad sign where Jeremy was concerned. Then on 22 August she phoned him while he was at his parents' house, at 2 am. Prior to the phone call he dreamed he was trapped in a dark house – afterwards that slimy ducks were spitting at him.

Over the next few days he had two more dreams which seemed to me to be clearly depicting what a mess he was in and his denial of it. 'I was driving an old car in an old sand pit where there was a deep pit followed by a steep winding slope to the top of a flat topped hill. I drove to the top several times, avoiding the danger. Then I went over the top. I managed to hold on to the car without causing any damage'. 'I was driving a car in snow on some hills. The snow became worse but although others were having difficulties, I was okay.'

There is at least a depiction of the serious situation he was in and Jeremy now acknowledged that the relationship had some serious consequences to it. But he used the dreams to justify his opinion that he could easily get out of them. He was completely unable to feel or see what a terrible mess he was in and that it was getting worse all the time. A dream of the 28 August made it even more clear how dangerous his situation was. He dreamed: 'Due to the sex I would grow initially then my body would slowly die.'

I took the dream very seriously but Jeremy chose instead

to go on holiday with M.(!) and did so two days later which was also the last time they made love — typical of the insiduous twists she would bring to the relationship. She simply told him on the first night of the holiday that she no longer wanted to have anything to do with him physically. After that he dreamed: 'I was at the seaside where M. and I were trying to get to the pier. I left her with a good friend who knew of me. She was saying how good things were. I ran and jumped, covering great distances downhill to the sea.'

The amount of denial in the dream is staggering — Jeremy is running ahead by leaps and bounds. M. is saying how good things are. It is particularly striking how the denial is being manifest in his dreams as well as in his attitude towards them. This reflects exactly his relationship with his parents — mutual denial. They chained him down with lies and deceit so that he could never surpass them and never be anything other than they imagined him to be. This is poignantly expressed in *An Attitude of Mind* by my friend, the poet, Bob Deveraux.[4]

Keep one foot in the grave
Obey your grandfather,
Chain yourself to the railings round his tomb,
Let him tap out his messages on the heel of your boot.
Ignore the dream drugged ideals of the youth,
Say that they are
Dream drugged
Gossamer
Fairy floating
Say that one day he will come down to earth;
And so he will,
For he is attached to you,
By an invisible cord,
Like a kite
And when the wind drops.
He will

Come
Down.
How can the child which you conceived,
Be wiser than his parents?
Do not follow where his fancy leads.
To follow is to risk death,
Or something worse.
Keep one foot in the grave.
To be half dead
Is to be half alive.

'What', asked Mark Tobey 'is the foe to our finding a voice
of our own? I should say fear. Fears, governed by public
opinion, by ideas of friends, by accepted patterns of traditional modes of thought'[5]

'From where' Tobey wrote, 'can release from all this
rigidity of pattern come? To me, it must come from the
Creative Life. That life which, drawing upon the vital forces
within us, gives us power to begin to think and feel for
ourselves, in our own individual way. The beginning of the
creative life is the beginning of faith in oneself, the will to
experience and order the phenomena about us.'

In Jeremy's case it became apparent that he could only
free himself from his problems if he freed himself from his
parents. He ceased to have contact with them and within a
short space of time began to show signs of improvement.
Divorcing himself from his parents was far from easy, particularly when others became angry and rejecting towards
him because of the stand he was taking. 'My brother, do you
want to go apart and be alone?' asked Nietzsche, 'Do you
want to seek the way to yourself? Pause just for a moment
and listen to me. He who seeks may easily get lost himself.
It is a crime to go apart and be alone.'

Sometimes radical choices do have to be made. If the
obstacle that blocks the Way is a person – if contact with
them is so negative or disturbing that you only suffer if you
see them, then obviously you need to question why you

have anything to do with them.

Change in therapy is largely effected by doing things differently. It is not a question of just talking; one actually has to actively set about changing your way of behaving. Many people go into therapy hoping that the therapist will change them without their changing so to speak. Change is often painful and difficult and a great deal of upset may need to be suffered along the Way. This is a lesson that the eminent psychoanalyst, Bruno Bettelheim, had to learn quickly in order to survive the horrors of Dachau and Buchenwald as he recounts in his book *The Informed Heart*:

'... up to the time I was imprisoned, I did not doubt the merit of psychoanalysis in general, and of my own in particular. I was convinced it had done as much for me as it could, and that no more was possible; so I had settled down, more or less uneasily, to live the way I then was, and I tried to like it ... The impact of the concentration camp on the other hand, within a few weeks, did for me what years of useful and quite successful analysis had not done.'

'Only dimly at first, but with even greater clarity, did I also come to see that how a man acts can alter what he is.'[6]

Most people find that they need to both strive to act differently and to analyse the impediments that stop them from doing so – whether they are internal or external. The exceptions are those people who basically just need someone they respect to confirm that their perceptions and intentions are appropriate or at the very least valid.

It isn't a question of blaming parents – as people often imagine – but of seeing things as they were or as they are. If the parents can do the same then there are immeasurable opportunities for growth in the relationship.

We all have our biases and blind spots but the ideal as a therapist is to see the patient as clearly as if one were a mirror that has been placed on the ground and that reflects back everything that is in front of it, exactly as it is. This is what Jeremy totally failed to do. The more he failed, the worse his life was. As we have seen, Jeremy saw whatever he wanted to in his dreams, just as his parents saw whatever they wanted to see in him. He saw whatever they wanted him to see in them, and from there it was an easy step to see whatever he wanted to see in M. or whatever she wanted him to see in her.

Subsequently he had a large number of dreams in which he was going downhill. On the 20 September he had a dream which seemed to show clearly how seriously he was being disturbed by the relationship which had ended some weeks before. It showed too how much trouble was in store for him: 'I was with someone on a hill. I saw some black smoke which formed clouds and then a hurricane/tornado. I told my friend to hold on. We lay on the grass waiting and the ground moved. I survived the hurricane.'

He realised that this dream meant that a terrible depression was on the way. Even so it wasn't until the first week of October that he became ill. He also crashed his car at the very moment that he thought of M. and as he put it, 'This was when I began to realise what I had done and how disturbed I was becoming.'

We need to remember that the patient can create as many and often far more difficulties to impede progress than the therapist. At the outset of the therapy many people are very confused and resentful if you don't see them as they want to be seen, or if you don't play the family games with them. So to balance up my overview I shall include an account that Jeremy has given of his therapy with me.

'The first year seems a long time ago; now I feel almost as if I am looking through a tunnel and just seeing a vague shape of me at the other end. My feelings towards you then were that you were only after my money and that what you were saying about me was not true ....

'Once I started my life on my own I found some stability (after leaving his wife) 'from my new base and my life was becoming more meaningful. I still thought I was OK. The facts were I was drinking a great deal, I had no social friends; the only relationships were those at work; I was gambling most of my money away. I had funny habits like collecting screws out of the gutter and not allowing myself substantial food ... and feeling immense guilt if ever I was out enjoying myself. In spite of this I still did not think I was in need of your therapy. In fact my delusionary self even thought I was capable of giving therapy. So I was in competition with you, fighting rather than learning from you. This attitude plus the belief that you were only interested in my money became stronger as I felt stronger. What I have since realised was that through your therapy I was getting stronger, and using that strength against you. This resulted in a disastrous relationship with a woman, during which I ignored the warnings from you and from my dreams. You helped me over the consequent emotional battering, but still my attitude towards you was the same. As a result I went downhill rapidly, and my relationship with you deteriorated still further. I was unable to communicate with you, I lost what little of myself I had found. I was distancing myself from everyone apart from my daughters, and used them to pass on my guilt and disturbance. Within the group therapy I was not contributing – only causing confusion and disruption. The final straw was when I attempted to destroy your Christmas. As a result you gave me the ultimatum to either change my attitude or cease therapy. For the first time I was really scared of what was going on and for the first time horrified of what I would do without your special sort of truth. Even so my feelings towards you were of hate and anger at what I thought was a cruel ultimatum that forced me to confront myself. But I realised I had a commitment to therapy and to myself to change. As I looked at myself I became more and more repulsed as I realised what I really was like, particularly in my grandiose attitude towards others and my only knowing how to take from, not to give to others. Over the next two years I began to realise how I really was with others, and for the first time I admitted I was disturbed. I was, for the first time, really ashamed of how I was. My attitude changed towards others as I increased my awareness and insight. But with these changes I became more aware of my hostility and deviousness towards you. I still have difficulties acknowledging these.

'As my awareness of myself and my behaviour towards others increased, my friendship and interests increased – my life became more meaningful. I began to experience more feelings about myself and about others. I feel that in the last two years I have shed more tears than in the rest of my life put together. These tears are for the regret over what I could have given and shared with those who loved me and also I think for relief at being released from the cocoon I had been trapped in over the years. As I look back to where I was at the beginning of treatment I am amazed at the doors you have opened up for me. I still have some distance to travel but at least now I am not deluded as to what I am or what I can be.'

'Anthony I see you as a sensitive, caring man with an extraordinary dedication to his patients. If it were not for you I do not believe I would be alive now. I will never be able to thank you enough.'

Of course sometimes what appears to be a serious backward step in therapy turns out to be the very opposite. I shall just mention two examples.

Jenny, the girl I mentioned earlier whose family got together to persuade her to go into a mental hospital, had received psychiatric treatment for years before seeing me. A lot of it centred on her relationship with her father which had involved regular anal intercourse from the time she was nine until she was fifteen. Jenny was a very sweet, frail timid little woman. I remember one of the first sessions. She said that there was no point in discussing the sex she had with her father, because she'd talked it over with countless psychiatrists. I pondered for a moment and asked if she really talked about it or if they just glossed over it. Suddenly as she opened her mouth to quietly answer my question, a deep booming male voice roared out from the depths of her being 'They just glossed over it'. She shook from head to foot and was horrified by this appalling sound that felt as if it belonged in the Exorcist. We came to look forward in a way to this voice emerging because it always confirmed that we had really got to the heart of the matter.

But I digress. I want to mention Jenny because she demonstrated magnificently the profound effect that can arise from re-enacting our memories. When Jenny came to see me she had given up all hope of having children. She was married – unhappily – but still desperately wanting a child. However her doctors were treating her for what they said was a severe thyroid difficulty and had told her she could never conceive. I always trust my intuition over these matters and felt and said most emphatically that I did not agree with them. I could feel nothing about her that indicated she had anything like a thyroid condition and I thought it was likely that her being unable to conceive was entirely psychosomatic and that it was tied up with her sexual relationship with her father – she didn't believe me.

Jenny made good progress. It was interesting to discover that she felt no real anger against her father. On the contrary she felt sorry for him and even felt glad that there had at least been that experience of closeness with him. But she felt enormous hatred towards her mother who she came to realise knew fully what was going on and who always contrived to be out of the room at convenient moments whenever he wanted sex. It suited the mother that things should be as they were. As she came to integrate these realisations Jenny changed considerably – the most dramatic change of all was that she became pregnant. Some months into the pregnancy she began to deteriorate and then went completely out of her mind. She found herself compelled to go to a hospital. She demanded treatment – but couldn't say what for – naturally they said they couldn't help. She became very distressed and created such a scene that she came close to being sectioned. But it dawned on her that she had been to the hospital before and that had been on the very same day of the year. Furthermore she had been there for a miscarriage.

Jenny had completely repressed, not only the memory of the miscarriage, but the whole experience of being pregnant. She then saw how ridiculous it was that her doctors had said she was incapable of conceiving. This was the turning point in her treatment. She developed into a very strong and independent but still warm and kind woman who had a beautiful baby. I was very moved when she wrote to me a few years later to say how wonderful life was for herself and her baby and to thank me for getting her 'out of spaghetti junction'.

Anniversaries often intrude in this way – the results can be devastating when no one understands what is going on. But though re-experiencing anniversaries can be dramatic and disturbing the consequences, if the experience is integrated with understanding and feeling, are always extremely beneficial. I must not omit to mention that positive anniversaries are also likely to be re-experienced.

Helen was an older woman who came to see me suffering from severe alopecia – her hair was falling out and her scalp itched to the point of driving her to distraction. She was a tiny vivacious woman, prodigiously intelligent. She was a true Renaissance figure who had mastered any activity that she chose to direct her attention to.

Like Jenny she had had treatment before. Her previous therapy had been with a famous analyst – the daughter of one of Freud's closest associates. Helen had never known her father and lost her mother when she was two. She was immensely grateful that her previous analysis had led to her recalling her mother taking her to a convent and leaving her with the nuns while she went out – she never returned.

Helen had been seeing me for a few weeks when she again mentioned this memory. I asked her to describe it in detail once more. She told me how she was taken to the convent – placed on a table – the suitcases on the floor around her – her mother left – she sat there happily swinging her legs – enjoying the company of the nuns. I pondered upon this, unable to grasp what it was that didn't ring true in this recollection. I find that the things patients say either fit snuggly inside me or they roll around like pebbles unable to find a resting place. No amount of conscious effort will provide a solution to the conundrum – I just have to trust that if I leave things to my unconscious then the answer, or at least the right question, will emerge. And suddenly it did. I realised that the whole ambience of the memory was wrong. It just didn't seem likely that a two-year-old would happily swing her legs around in the company of complete strangers – whether they were nuns or not – while her mother went off and left her. Despite feeling some resistance to doing so, I told Helen what had gone through my mind. The resistance is usually an internalisation of the patients' feelings about the issue.

That night, for a few hours, Helen went mad. My questioning her recollection had profoundly affected her and she had plunged in the evening after the session, down into a nightmare memory of being in the tiny flat with her mother – a boyfriend of her mother's was there. Her mother and the boyfriend argued – a fight ensued. The next thing she remembered was her mother being dead on the floor and she – at two years old, spending the whole night trying to look after her Mummy and make her better. Eventually she made so much noise that a neighbour came to her assistance.

Over the following months strange symptoms developed. Helen had always loved red wine but suddenly it made her vomit. This happened for some days until she had a memory of kissing her dead mother and of blood shooting into her mouth. The vomiting stopped.

Later she developed terrible back pains. The pains would come and go in accordance with the issues that she talked about in her therapy. So we both assumed that the pains were psychosomatic. Later they became so intense that she sometimes had to leave the session. During this period there slowly emerged a memory of her rushing up to protect her mother by attacking the man who was hitting her. He pushed her violently so that she hit her head against a table edge and was knocked unconscious. She came to some time later to find her mother lying dead next to her. Eventually she decided to see an osteopath. Fortunately she chose a particularly brilliant practitioner. He examined her and told her that when she was two years old she suffered a violent assault, had been unconscious for some time and that during that experience her back had been badly damaged. Unfortunately Helen's treatment was stopped prematurely. Even so, one particularly positive benefit of it was that her son became transformed from a mediocre student to being able to choose a place at any university in the country.

No one – least of all themselves – could have predicted that either of these women had such dreadful experiences locked away inside them. No theory can encompass the infinite possibilitie. of human experience. It isn't knowledge that enables such things to emerge – but an open heart and an open mind. If the therapist endeavours to clear his mind of all prejudices and expectations then there is a chance that one day he will become a mirror free of distortions. Then whoever looks into it will see themselves reflected back exactly as they are.

CHAPTER SIX

Hymn To Apollo

To open the eternal worlds, to open the immortal
Eyes of Men inwards into the worlds of Thought:
into Eternity.

Blake

Only Zeus was more majestic than his son, Apollo. In Ancient times the Greeks regarded the shrine to Apollo that stood at Delphi as the centre of the world, marking the spot with the Omphalos or navel stone.

'Know thyself' was the inscription that Apollo's shrine conveyed to the suppliants. It was there that the Pythia, the prophetess, would fall into a trance and become the divine instrument of the great God. It is this imagery of direct inspiration that I set in opposition to the Echo-Maker in the title of this book.

This much is fairly common knowledge. Much less well known is that the Greek God, Apollo, may have originated with the British Druids. Not only that but there were various Bards — the *awenyddion* who, like Pythia, went into a frenzied trance uttering obscure prophetic messages.

It is something of a commonplace to trace the origins of psychotherapy back to the confessional. Occasionally, as with Jung, one finds references to the diagnostic use of dreams by the Ancient Greeks. It is certainly true that dreams were often decisive in the Ancient World. Joscelyn Godwin, in his book *Mystery Religions in the Ancient World* wrote, 'The Greater Mysteries, or higher grades of initiation, were conducted individually rather than collectively. The initiations of Isis were given to those priests or laity selected by the goddess through having had significant dreams. Sometimes the dream

itself might be the initiation: the late Platonist Damascius
dreamed "I had become Attis and the Great Mother was
celebrating the Hilaria (feast of Cybele) in my honour (Vita
Isidori 131). From this he acquired the certitude of eternal
salvation." '1

The Druids had long used dreams as a means of making
major decisions. Ward Rutherford, in his book *Celtic Mythology* tells how 'in Ireland, when the king died, the royal
Druids assembled, sacrificed an ox, made a broth of its flesh,
then slept on its skin. In the dream that followed, the identity
of the future king would be revealed.'2

In fact the significance of the British Mystical tradition
was recognised in Classical times. The Greeks learnt of the
Celts in about 500 BC. By this time the Bards had taken over
the functions of the Druids to the point where the terms
'Bard' and 'Druid' were interchangeable. Pliny the Elder, in
his *Natural History* called them Magicians and said that the
Druids acted as if magic had been invented in Britain. Diog-
enes Laertius put the Druids on the same level as the Persian
Magi and the most advanced Indian Yogis.

So who were the Druids? Anne Ross and Don Robins
give this succinct account of the Druid's role in Celtic Society
in their recent book *The Life and Death of a Druid Prince*.
'The Druids were concerned with divine worship, the due
performance of sacrifices public and private, the interpretation
of ritual questions, settlement of disputes and the punishment
of those who refused to accept their ruling. Caesar asserts
that Druid power originated in Britain and that Britain
remained the centre of Druidism.

'The Druids taught their acolytes the Druidical secrets
by word of mouth. They chanted the lessons to their students,
who sang them back to their masters until they knew them
by heart. In their judicial function of settling disputes, the
Druids determined the amount of damages due to the
wronged parties. Their role in determining succession was
crucial, as the early vernacular tradition of Ireland makes clear.
There were constant boundary disputes requiring Druidic

intervention. In Gaul, those who disobeyed Druidic decisions were banished from the tribe or the wider community, and there are hints in Caesar's writing that they were in danger of becoming sacrificial victims, fuel for the Beltain fires.'[3]

As the Druids came under increasing persecution the Bardic tradition increasingly took over. It took twenty years to train to be a Bard. The British Bards put the title *ollave* meaning something like doctor, before their name, and this was so, even up to the time of Cromwell. They were trained in poetry, mythology, story telling, astrology, herbalism, the development of psychic faculties, magic, hypnotism and the interpretation of dreams. The Bards were held in such high esteem that no one, not even a king, could refuse to give a gift if a Bard requested it, to the point where one king put his eye out to fulfil such a request. Nor could a king speak until the Druid or Bard had spoken first. On a more mundane level they were exempt from taxes.

These associations are still very much in people's minds. At a time when I knew nothing of these things, a patient dreamed of herself as sitting at a table in an old castle with me as a Merlin figure standing behind her. Another patient dreamed of walking along by the sea with me as an old man dressed in the traditional white robes of the Druids.

The Druids and Bards used dreams in a number of significant ways: for healing, for prophesy and as a means of communicating with other worlds. Sadly in our own times the scientific materialist reductionist outlook, particularly that of Freud, has led to the virtual loss of this status and has replaced it with a perverted view of their significance. It must be said that Jung was a noticeable exception to this lamentable failing. He was, for instance, able to predict the outbreak of the Second World War on the basis of his patients' dreams, and placed particular significance upon dreams such as one that he had of his wife after her death, which he understood as a direct communication from her.

Freud, however, had this to say in the *Introductory Lectures on The Censorship of Dreams*: 'The purpose against which the dream-censorship is directed must be described in the first instance from the point of view of that agency itself. If so, one can only say that they are invariably of a reprehensible nature, repulsive from the ethical, aesthetic and social point of view – matters of which one does not venture to think at all or only with disgust ... The ego, freed from all ethical bonds, also finds itself at one with all the demands of sexual desire, even those which have long been condemned by our aesthetic upbringing and those which contradict all the requirements of moral restraint. The desire for pleasure – 'the libido', as we call it – chooses its objects without inhibition and by preference, indeed, the forbidden ones: not only other men's wives, but above all incestuous objects, objects sanctified by the common agreement of mankind, a man's mother and sister, a woman's father and brother. Lusts which we think of as remote from human nature show themselves strong enough to provoke dreams. Hatred, too, rages without restraint. Wishes for revenge and death directed against those who are nearest and dearest in waking life, against the dreamer's parents, brothers and sisters, husband or wife, and his own children are nothing unusual. These censored wishes appear to rise up out of a positive Hell. After they have been interpreted when we are awake, no censorship of them seems to us too severe.[4]

While I wouldn't for a moment deny that these are elements in everyone's dream life it really seems to me to be tragic that such a narrow, cynical, uninspired, depreciatory, contemptuous, reductionist view of our dream life has been allowed to hold sway. Ward Rutherford, in *The Druids*, explained:- 'More than anyone, the shaman can claim to a vocation: that it is shamanism that chooses him, not he it. Impelled by some power he cannot resist, often a succession of dreams, he withdraws from the society of his fellows to live in the wild, where, fasting and meditating, he lays himself open as it were to the very forces imminent in his natural surroundings.

'Soon he will become prey to terrible visitations. He may believe himself to be undergoing many incarnations in the space of a few nights, culminating in some dreadful act of symbolical self-immolation. At least he will reach stasis and his own ultimate reward – a total union with the Cosmos. As well as the spirits of the dead, he will have emerged from his trauma in touch with "all the spirits of earth and sky and sea" in the words of Rosmussen's informant who was himself a shaman. From now on all these will be his guides and helpers.

'Thus reborn, his first companions will be other shamans who recognise him as one fit to share their secrets: those of animal and bird life, of cloud and climate; stars and their motion; herbs and their properties. But above all, he will learn the great myths which are the history of his people.

'When he returns to the midst of his fellow men, probably under a new name as token of his regeneration, they will quickly recognise that he is a different person, the recipient of special widsom. At one with nature and the elements, he may now choose for his habitat some remote place in the forest and it's here he will have to be sought for consultation....

'Certainly in shamanism we have a system of belief whose lineage stretches back perhaps 20,000 years. Something very close to it existed among the inhabitants of Scandinavia as early as Neolithic times. Its effect on the Druids is obvious and it's virtually certain that there were shamans among the Indo-Europeans before the great migrations'.[5]

The anthropologist, Francis Huxley, recalled in his obituary on Laing in *The Guardian* that Laing invited him, in the sixties, to join the *Philadelphia Association.* 'He did so because of my interests as a social anthropologist in such things as shamanism, which I had recently come into.'

As Laing has written in *The Transcendental Experience* 'One of the difficulties of talking in the present day of these matters is that the very existence of inner realities is now called into question.

'By "inner" I mean our ways of seeing the "external", "objective" presence – imagination, dreams, phantasies, trances, the realities that modern man, for the most part, has not the slightest direct awareness of.'[6]

Laing's interest in these matters arose from several sources: his own experiences, the accounts of some of his patients, particularly some of those who would be diagnosed as schizophrenic, who felt that they were going through a spiritual journey; and from his reading about and experience of, other cultures, particularly with regard to Shamanism. Obviously the Druids didn't just appear out of nowhere. They originated from the wandering tribes of Southern Russia – the Indo-Europeans.

Ward Rutherford has this to say about the origins of Druidism.[7] He is writing of the 'propitiatory rituals' to ensure a good hunt that would be 'carried out by each or any member of the group of hunters. It gives place to one wherein, the social units having increased in size and complexity, this becomes the responsibility of an expert. He is the shaman, able to throw himself into trances in which he can enter the land of the Spirits, communicate with its inhabitants and hence on his return dictate the rituals necessary not merely to banish those which are malign causing illness or other misfortunes, but also with the help of his personal tutelary spirits to invoke the aid of others both powerful and well disposed,

'The word "shaman" is derived from the language of the Tungas peoples of Siberia, among whom he is still to be found practising, as he is among the nomadic herdsman and hunters of Northern Europe, the Arctic and the plains of north-east Asia....

Francis Huxley, writing in *The Guardian*, said, 'Laing, there is no doubt, had the shamanic temperament and recognised the fact. This gift, which so often begins as a disorder, is not recognised as such in western psychiatry, which therefore cannot use its therapeutic advantages: a fact which of course underlines so much of Laing's writings on "anti-psychiatry" which amounts to no less than what psychiatry should be doing if it truly understood the facts of the case'.[8]

In *Celtic Mythology* Rutherford says of the shaman that 'In particular, he acquires the gift of inducing trances in which he can leave his mortal body. It is this last capacity that defines him, though as a kind of bonus – signalling his special relationship with the supernatural – the shaman also gains the gift of prophesy, clairvoyance, and clairaudience.'

Rutherford adds that he is also a healer 'But with his unique personal knowledge of the Other World, when any member of the community dies it is for him to guide his or her spirit to its new resting place. That is to say, he is communal psychopomp or conductor of souls.'

On a day by day basis the shaman enjoys the most intimate relationship with nature. 'However, the shaman does not merely imitate birds or animals: he is credited with the ability to transform himself into them. Chukchee and Eskimo shamans can turn themselves into wolves.... The fact that during his trance the Shaman's soul, as it were, takes flight means that it is often likened to a bird, especially the high soaring eagle.'[9]

In *The Elements of Shamanism* Neville Drury points out the 'Ceremonial ritual is the outer enactment of an internal event. In all religions and also in shamanism and ceremonial magic, those performing a ritual believe that what they are doing is not simply theatrical but accords with some sort of sacred, inner reality – that for a time they are caught up in a mystical drama, perhaps involving union with a god, identification with a source of spiritual healing or the act of embodying some sort of transcendent power. In such a way the shaman, priest, or magician believes he is tapping into a dimension which is much larger and more awesome than the world of familiar reality. It is very much a case of participating in a mystery – of leaving the everyday realm and, for a sacred and special period of time, entering the Cosmos.

Many anthropologists and sociologists have a problem with this. Because they are trained to record external events in details, to monitor behaviour patterns and the ways in which such behaviour proves meaningful in the social matrix, they are often inclined to believe that that is all that is happening.

Shamanism is no exception. To many observers the shaman is little more than an exotic performer, a person who, through evocative and stimulating ritual is able to induce a state of hysteria which deludes both himself and his audience.'[10]

Now it would seem to be easy to argue that the shamanistic concern with natural energy forces has no relevance for modern psychiatry and psychotherapy. If you think that, you couldn't be more wrong. In *R. D. Laing — The Man and His Ideas* by Richard Evans, Laing had this to say; 'It has been discovered that fields of energy on this planet are extensions of the furthest blips picked up on the astronomer's telescope; the molecular structure of human cells vibrates in some way with the vibrations from outer stellar space. Our whole body is not primarily bounded by skin, but is part of a continuum of geophysical fields. Gay Luce's book, *Body Time* describes work on disturbed patients in Canadian mental hospitals in which they tried to find all the variables, including interpersonal ones, the staff going off and coming on, diet, medications and so on. They attempted to correlate these variables with sudden outbursts of violence observed in some of the patients and they couldn't find any correlations at all. When they fed the information to a space-research data processing unit, they found exact correlations with certain geophysical storms, like sunspots, to which some people seem to respond more sensitively than others. Lunatics take their name from the moon. We know the moon affects organic life and the phasing and maturation of organic processes. It affects all the waters of the earth. In the tides, an enormous amount of water moves up and down with the moon. Over 80 per cent of our body is made of water, and it seems inevitable that our fluids are going to be affected by such things as the moon. That's not Cranksville; that's perfectly ordinary common sense.'[11]

We can be sensitive to many such forces. For instance,

some years ago I dreamed that I was standing by a huge rock. Suddenly things started flying all over the place and I immediately knew that I would have to flee or die! I tried to make sense of the dream but couldn't fathom it at all. Then the next day I learned of the terrible earthquake in Mexico.

As was mentioned earlier the initiation of a shaman can come about through dreams. The following is an account of a series of dreams that profoundly changed my view of life and of myself. They occurred in May 1987. One of the fascinating things about them is that I wouldn't have realised their significance had a patient of mine not gone to the *Festival of Mind and Body*. There he heard a talk in which the speaker said that some weeks previously, on 11 May, there had been a massive influx of energy that hit the Earth and that was profoundly associated with psychic awareness. My patient was very struck by this because, having a deep interest in psychic issues, he had been very affected by such matters being discussed for the whole of a group therapy session on that very day, 11 May.

This was the first time that such issues had been broached in the eighteen months of the group's existence. I must say that I didn't know what to make of it, but I was as impressed as my patient had been by its corresponding to what was a very powerful group experience for all concerned. That night I decided to look up my dreams for 11 May and the days around it to see if there were any references to this phenomena in them. I was shocked to discover that I had dreamed a series of dreams that meant next to nothing to me at the time but which now took on a meaning that I found awe-inspiring.

On 7 May I dreamed that an enormous nuclear bomb had been dropped on London but to my amazement it did no damage at all.

On 10 May I dreamed of a shadow of a blackbird coming towards me and turning into a magnificent eagle soaring over mountains.

On 11 May I dreamed that I poured liquid on a dying plant which immediately grew and flowered at an amazing rate — I tried to draw a patient's attention to this but he was unimpressed. In a second dream I was living in a secluded hovel — strange things were going on. I was chosen to play in a game for which I was totally unprepared and had to borrow kit from the opposition.

On 12 May I dreamed of an enormous number of huge red balloons falling out of the sky and bombarding the Thames.

With hindsight I can see that on the 7 May I was already sensing this massive influx of energy (which I have since discovered other commentators on such issues have referred to). The speaker had emphasised the inspirational and trans- formative effect of this energy, which is clearly depicted in my dream of 10 May with the blackbird being transformed into a magnificent eagle (the shaman's soul) — which always represents for me the mind and spirit. This transformative effect is also depicted in the plant being revived. I feel here that the plant represents myself — that part of me that had suffered as a result of my lack of willingness to acknowledge most psychic issues. Then, in the second dream, living in a hovel portrays me as the reclusive shaman but also shows how isolated I was from these issues. In the dream I know that strange things are going on and I am involved in something for which I am totally unprepared — which was clearly the case. Having to borrow my kit from the oppo- sition — that is from people like the speaker, who I really did regard as the opposition. The dream of 12 May makes what I feel to be obvious reference to the energy coming from the sky.

I was permanently changed by this experience. This change was depicted in a dream that actually occurred before my patient informed me of this matter on 30 May. I dreamed on 21 May that 'Although I know intellectually that it is not to be, I am forced to accept that the Holy Grail is a living reality in my family.'

I feel very strongly that the dream depicts my being involved in a spiritual quest. That it was portending the unfolding of my shamanic abilities. Which brings me back to the second dream of 11 May. What does it mean that I am chosen to play in a game? Who or what has done the choosing?

Shortly after this I had a dream that was wholly shamanic in its ambience and in the activity portrayed, 'I have found the area in which life, death, fantasy and the unconscious meet. There is a very strange atmosphere like that in Cocteau's Orpheus. I am being chased with others through corridors by the Devil — I turn and face him and see that he has no more power than I.' Here we can see clear reference to the shamanic journey into other worlds.

The following day I dreamed that I was under attack from UFOs. Then two days later, on the 28 May I dreamed that I met Segovia and that he took me into his room to give me a private lesson. It was clear that what he had to teach me was very special.

And just to jump a day, on 30 May I dreamed that Jung was talking to me for an extended period of time. I shall return to these dreams.

On 29 May I dreamed that I was with my father and sister — planes were whizzing by, as in the fight scenes in Battle Star Galactica — there were incredible views and angles — but my father was oblivious to it all. My father is heavily rationalistic and not open to psychic matters — but he also seems to represent that part of myself that was resistant to them.

It was on 30 May that my patient spoke to me about the lecture at the Festival of Mind and Body, the same morning that I woke up having dreamed of Jung talking to me. Jung himself would have undoubtedly seen this as meaning that this was an actual communication.

I now wish to return to the Segovia dream of 28 May. On 5 June I learnt from a patient that Segovia had died on 3 June. Because I don't read newspapers or listen to the news, this was the first that I'd heard of it. Again, having remembered the dream in which I met Segovia, I decided to look up my dreams for that time. In the following dream sequence the role of the shaman as someone who accompanies a person through death is graphically depicted.

On the same night as the private lesson dream – 28 May – I also dreamed that there was a weird and dangerous situation – and that everyone had to stay in their own area.

On 31 May I had a revolting dream about malfunctioning human intestines which I now see related to the failure of Segovia's body as he died, and to the Shamanic experience of dismemberment.

On 1 June I dreamed of Peter Ustinov dying – physically he bears some resemblance to Segovia. On the day that Segovia died there were several occasions when I was convinced that my heart was going to stop and thus that I would die. This struck me as very odd at the time, since I was and am very healthy. On the day I learnt of Segovia's death, I had woken with a dream in which several of my teeth fell out at once and there was a terrible sense of ageing and loss.

Clearly on 28 May I dreamed that I was in a dangerous situation and that everyone had to stay in their own area because I was sensing the confusion of identity with Segovia – and experiencing his death myself.

This raises the very interesting point of how can we be sure that what we dream of has anything to do with ourselves at all? The answer is that we can't.

On the night that Segovia died I had a very disturbed night's sleep. Throughout the night I repeatedly heard the last few bars of Segovia's recording of the Manuel Ponce guitar concerto. This was punctuated with visual dreams. But let me first say that the music I dreamed of is particularly joyful – a fact which I found profoundly moving and meaningful since it seemed to me to be an expression of how Segovia felt at the very end of his life – a joyful message about death. I recall too that I was very affected by reading an account of Segovia saying goodbye to the dying Manuel Ponce, one of his oldest and dearest friends, with the two of them knowing that they would never see each other again.

The visual dreams were firstly, that Julian Bream was very upset, and secondly, there was again a dreadful ambience in the dream like that in Cocteau's *Orpheus*. I was walking through somewhere like an enormous hospital with no beds but with the floor covered in dead and dying people.

At the time I analysed the dreams and then forgot them – they didn't really mean much to me. But now I could understand why I dreamed of the guitarist Julian Bream being so upset. I remembered him looking like that when I once saw him pacing the streets before a concert, shortly after his having heard that a close friend had committed suicide.

Then there was the hospital which takes on an uncanny significance. It is as if all those who were dead and dying exist on the same plane. What was most disturbing about the dream was that they were just left on the floor like so much rubbish. The dream bothered me a lot at the time but it worried me a lot more when I realised Segovia was dead or dying whilst I dreamed it. This experience affected me very deeply.

Then just over two weeks later I had another dream which took things further still. On 22 June I dreamed that I was giving a session to an old lady – suddenly I was taken over by a horrifying psychic state and I started screaming at her 'You're dying – you're dying'. I woke up and got up – it was some time before I was able to go back to bed again.

The next day I felt that I should play Verdi's *Requiem* – which I did – loudly – because for some reason, which at the time I felt very bad about, I wanted the old lady next door to listen to it. Later I repeatedly heard her saying in my mind 'Now I know who you are.' It wasn't until the next day that I heard that she committed suicide at the very time of my dream.

The shamanic function is an essential aspect of Laing's personal approach to psychotherapy and psychiatry. But he recognised that it was a role that was by no means suitable for everyone. None the less he wrote in *The Transcendental Experience* 'among physicians and priests there should be some

who are guides, who can educate the person from this world
and induct him to the other. To guide him in it; and to lead
him back again'.[12]

There are difficulties about discussing issues relating to
shamanic experiences in psychotherapy. Laing makes reference to some of these in *Recessions and Regressions* in *The
Voice of Experience*, without question his most closely and
elegantly argued work. 'This ordinary world would be unrec-
ognisable without our standard distinctions of here-there,
now-then, inner-outer, me-not me. Nevertheless the world
continually transgresses these and all distinctions. Here, there
and everywhere, the world is not divided as we divide it.

'Words cannot express adequately modes of experience
where the distinctions enshrined by language do not exist.
What cannot be put into words cannot be said in words.'[13]

'Regression is usually construed as a defence; against, it
has been variously suggested, the frustrations of outer reality,
against ambivalence, against overwhelming hatred. It is often
said that it occurs especially in people with weak ego boundaries, who suffer from a psychopathological disability to give
and receive love.

'These points have been reiterated ad nauseam in the self-
styled "literature" on the subject.'[14]

Thus many approaches to therapy outlaw experiences
that are essential for growth.

Andrew Collier in *R. D. Laing — The Philosophy and Politics
of Psychotherapy* begins his book with this anecdote about
Laing which describes the attitude which is the precondition
for being able to fulfil the shamanic role in therapy; 'I was
once at a lecture given by R. D. Laing, at which he was asked
what the differences of method were between the various
schools of analytical psychotherapy — Freudian, Kleinian, etc.
He replied, as I remember, that there were no differences of
method, only of terminology; for instance, in the course of
an analysis by a Kleinian, the word 'Breast' might be used a
hundred times more than in an orthodox Freudian analysis,
while the orthodox Freudian would use the word 'penis' and

'vagina' a hundred times more. Laing was then asked what words he would use more than other analysts, and he said he would be inclined to use the same words as the other person (who was being analysed).[15]

Only if the therapist has this relationship to what is being said to him and to the other person who is saying it, will he be able to give his patient the confidence to follow their train of thought wherever it might lead them.

At the very end of *The Voice of Experience* Laing narrates one of his unmatchable vignettes. One of the fascinating aspects of this case history is that it manifests so many of the traditional shamanistic elements, particularly with the woman involved becoming an animal. Laing mentions a hound but I suspect a wolf was more likely to have been the case. It is one of his most priceless, hauntingly evocative accounts of an experience of therapy with him. What is particularly important to me is the lesson which Laing offers that 'the distinction between possibility and impossibility is usually among the first to go' and the openmindedness that this leads me to have towards the next thing that my next patient will say to me.

I begin the case history about the halfway point: 'She came to see me for an hour once a fortnight and talked about her life, while I listened and said very little. In her dreams she came alive, she even had orgasms, the first since her electric shocks. But while she was awake she remained dead.

'It was Good Friday. She lived in a remote country house. It was empty until Monday. She was expecting nobody.

'At three o'clock in the afternoon she was meandering aimlessly through the house when a fierce white heat began to pierce the middle of her back behind her solar plexus, to burn and spiral into her, to spread through her and begin to take her over. It was the Spirit of Life and Love. It was Christ. It was the same as ten years ago. She had a few seconds to decide whether to resist (she felt if she did she would perish), or to go along with it (if she did she might go mad).

'She decided to go along with it. As soon as she made

that decision, she became calm and lucid. She observed that she was not moving herself, but that she was being moved from her solar plexus. She looked on calmly as she was moved to go to a bedroom and bring down a blanket, to make a lair as for a dog under the kitchen table. Why she was moved to do that, she had no idea at the time.

'When she had prepared her lair, she found herself taking off her clothes. She looked on as she turned into a hound, on hands and knees, or rather paws. She could not speak or walk. She growled and prowled around the house until it was dark, when she prowled down to a cellar she had not entered for years. With difficulty she opened the door with her snout, and huddled up in a far corner, naked, cold, in pitch darkness, feeling rats, eventually, running over her. She had lost all idea of time.

'After, she knew not how long, but while it was still, she thought later, the same night, she found herself prowling from the far corner of the cellar, up to an attic. A full moon shone in through the open window. Bathed in moonlight, she placed her front paws on the window sill and howled to the moon. Then she had to prowl back down to her place in the cellar again, and stay huddled as before in the rat-infected blackness.

'She had to repeat this whole procedure two more times, three times in all. After the third time, huddled in the cellar, a warm drowsiness came over her, and she fell asleep. When she awoke she was still a hound. She prowled out of the cellar. It was still night, but she had no idea which night. She prowled to the lair under the kitchen table, snuggled into it, was quickly once more overcome with a pleasant warm drowsiness, and fell asleep again.

'When she awoke it was dawn. She was a naked lady curled up in a blanket under the kitchen table. She arose, It was Easter Monday. She felt – all right. She has never felt dead again. She has never been excessive again.... There is method in this madness. The whole episode is perfectly timed with mythic time (Easter, Good Friday to Monday, death

and resurrection) and the demands of her ordinary life....
Afterwards, she felt herself to be (as she had almost given up
hope she ever would again) an ordinary woman.'[16]

Precognition dreams are more generally accepted. One
morning I awoke having dreamed that a maniac opened fire
with a machine gun at the entrance to an underground tunnel.
Many people were brutally killed. I awoke feeling very uneasy
after the dream. Although I was very keen to go to London
that day and got ready to leave, I suddenly decided to stay
at home and not to go to Kings Cross as planned. It was that
evening that the Kings Cross disaster took place.

Dreams that involve a self-protective function are easy
to account for. Less easy is the following experience. One
night I awoke having had two dreams. The first involved an
empty warehouse. In the second I dreamed that I couldn't
bear to look at the horribly scarred face of a soldier – there
were stitches all over it.

The next evening my first patient spent the bulk of his
session talking about an empty warehouse, and my next
patient, whom I hadn't seen before, replied in answer to my
question as to whether she had any nightmares, that they
were about her sister's boyfriend whose body is horribly
scarred by an air crash. When she dreams of him she can't
bear to look at his body. As Lao Tzu said:

> Without going outside, you may know the whole
>   world.
> Without looking through the window, you may see
>   the way of heaven.
> The further you go, the less you know.
> Thus the sage knows without travelling;
> He sees without looking;
> He works without doing.[17]

CHAPTER SEVEN

Recapitulation

The only commentator in the analytic literature who has really appreciated the significance of the relationship between psychotherapy and Shamanism is Jung's co-worker, Louise von Franz. She wrote, 'the earliest origins of modern psychotherapy known to history lie in archaic shamanism'.[1]

'To be able to see the spirits whether awake or in dreams is the most important part of the Shaman's vocation.'[2]

'Jung's report of his experience after separating from Freud strikes one as being an astonishing parallel to the form of primeval experience of the spirit world. Its "journey to the beyond" occurred in middle life. Jung had dreams until the recurring motif of the dead from the historical past coming to life or of a dove, transformed into a little girl, coming to him as a messenger from the realm of the dead.'[3]

'As a shaman often suffers from the plight of his people so Jung was afflicted by dreams of blood baths and catastrophes in Europe.... He decided to take the journey to the beyond "Suddenly it was as though the ground literally gave way beneath my feet, and I plunged down into dark depths." '[4]

'The symbolic inner experiences which the Shaman lives through during his period of initiation are identical with the symbolic experiences the man of today lives through during the individuation process'[5]

Unfortunately von Franz's work is one of the least read books on Jung — she is perhaps too erudite. None the less she is astonishingly sensitive to the issues involved and touches upon matters that follow Jungians, such as Storr, let alone most psychoanalysts, are very much averse to. For instance she observes that the shaman 'heals the sufferer by means of his own trance....'[6]

This is a critical point that I have already quoted Jung on – that the psychotherapist cures by his ability to confront the same issues and psychic factors that the patient has to face. It is often precisely his willingness to do this and his ability to do so that is the main curative factor.

Von Franz wrote, 'curing the soul of individuals and collective states of possession is really the principal task of the Shaman. If an ordinary man meets a demon or a spirit – that is, psychologically, an archetypal content of the unconscious – he will be possessed by it and therefore fall ill. The same thing often happens to a Shaman during his period of initiation but he knows how to free himself and cure himself by means of the right kind of behaviour in relation to the spirit world. That enables him to help ordinary sufferers who cannot help themselves.'[7]

Von Franz hit the nail on the head where her assessment of what is unique to Jung was concerned. These are the qualities that he shared with Laing. Thus one can say that the reason that Laing and Jung stood head and shoulders above other therapists of their generation was because they were Shamans – and yet many therapists, particularly psychoanalysts, view precisely what made them so great as an aberration. Both men, for instance, have been labelled schizophrenic by those who were opposed to them. Storr's remarks show how great is the divide between the shamanic and the analystic standpoints.

It is in the nature of things that most therapists are not Shamans, nor could many of them be, even if they wanted to. None the less a great deal can be gained from adapting a shamanic outlook. In essence this means not seeing or creating differences where they don't exist, and this in itself leads to a profound sense of openness to experience and the experiences of others. But here we have a problem – the very word for analysis means to dissect, to decompose, to break down. An analystic approach to therapy is often used as an attack upon experience for the benefit of the analyst rather than that of the patient. Laing quotes instances of this in *The Voice of Experience.* What is needed is that sense of unity that Bernard Leach described in his poem, *The Wave* — which he was inspired to write when looking out to sea from his house in St. Ives:-

It stood up on end
And said
Lazy bones
And head
Come out and play
Come forth and dance. It waved
I waved
Everything Waved[8]

Appendix

Earlier this year I asked Ronnie Laing if he would allow me to interview him for the journal, *International Minds*. His would have been the first in a series of interviews that includes Laurens Van der Post, Yehudi Menuhin and His Holiness the Dalai Lama. Ronnie declined the offer. However he asked me if I had realised what a valuable project it would be to have a book consisting of interviews with such 'Citizens of the World'. Further, although he had largely ceased giving interviews, he volunteered to provide me with the first one for the book. We were to meet in September, but then he changed his plans completely and we met instead in July. Myself and a patient of mine, who was a close friend, each had a therapy session with him on the same day, and then the three of us went to have lunch. We were the last people to have therapy with him in this country.

We went to one of my favourite restaurants, *La Loggia* in Edgware Road, and we sat down to discuss the book. After half an hour he suddenly announced that he would give the interview there and then. This came as a shock, not least because it meant that I had to go out and buy a tape recorder in the middle of my meal! With hindsight I understood that unconsciously, if not consciously, Ronnie knew that he was dying and that if he didn't give me the interview at that moment then it would never take place. The interview was only half complete and the plan was that it would be finished over the phone when he returned from the holiday during which he died.

Although the interview is shorter than I would have wished, there are some fascinating moments in it. In some respects it has very much the flavour of a last statement. The following, then, are a few extracts from this conversation.

Me· When I've heard you give lectures you appear, in many respects, to be more concerned to move people than you are to inform them, whereas most psychiatrists are usually intent upon letting people know how knowledgeable they are. It seems to me that you look for a gut reaction – that you want them to be emotionally affected by what you say. Which is very similar to a musical experience.

Laing: Well a great number of the things that I've written about and talk about entail what I call realisation. Realisation is when you actually sense and know that you know what you know. That you know in a realising way. For instance, the guy who came to see me about thirty years ago now. He felt like killing himself. He was very depressed and despairing and so on. He didn't know why. There wasn't enough in his family history to account for it. Sometime after – about three months – when he was going over and over why it might be that he felt like that, he suddenly burst into tears, cried for about five minutes and then, as that sort of crying often does, it suddenly stopped. He heaved several sighs and then said that he had never REALISED before that he was a human being. He had suddenly realised that he was a human being, and that it was basically in that moment he felt he had come across what it was that was troubling him. He didn't feel that life was worth living. He didn't even feel that he was a human being in the first place. He was going to find out whether it would be worth living while feeling that he was a human being but he hadn't found that out yet. He completely changed at that moment. Well I talk about that as a very simple thing that most people, like you and me, and her (pointing to the different people at the table) and so on take for granted. I examine 'who are you' and 'who is she' and 'who is me'. When you actually stay with that for some while people become very moved. Because they get in touch with all of the things that these things actually do mean to them. They mean a great deal to everyone.

Me: You know the Indian idea of Darshan. Do you feel that you have that effect upon people?

Laing: I don't feel that I have that effect upon people – particularly – one way or the other. But I am quite often told by people that it has made a big difference to their lives that they have met me.

Me: How are you affected when they say that?

Laing: Well it's a very gratifying thing to hear – so I'm very pleased to hear it. And it is a very nice thing to feel that you are the sort of person that has got a sort of grace – that one might have of that order. That is a very nice thought. It's one of the effects that I have. Say if you asked them to tell me more. They say 'You've given me permission to be and you don't seem to be playing any numbers on me. Do you realise Dr Laing, how rare that is? I've gone to see twenty people or one hundred people and believe me, I'm telling you, I've never met anybody like you – who is not making any numbers. You let me be and you understand me – not making a big deal about seeming to understand me. So thank you Dr Laing just for being.'

Me: Do you get that all over the world?

Laing: Yes. I think that my books up to but not including *The Facts of Life* are, in America in particular, still for

most people the books that people associate with the
name R D Laing and I've even heard the expression,
'classical Laing'.

Me: How did you feel about 'Laingian' being included in
the Oxford Dictionary?

Laing: What?

Me: Laingian becoming a word?

Laing: Oh is it?

Me: Didn't you know that?

Laing: No I didn't.

Me: Oh yes, I was quite impressed by that.

Laing: Yah.

Me: It's in the supplement.

Laing: What is a Laingian?

Me: Someone who adheres to the principals of R D Laing.

Laing: Oh

Me: Well I thought that was quite a feather in your cap.
Particularly for someone who appreciates language.

Laing: Yeh. I think the other two things – my portrait is
hanging up in the Scottish National Portrait gallery –
between Mary, Queen of Scots and John Knox. That
was done about six years ago. That was a very nice
gesture, compliment, from the trustees. And I've got

one of the longest entries in the *Compendium on Mind*, which is a standard reference book, bigger than Freud.

I'd like to feel that I'm the sort of person that Nietzsche would have been glad to have met if he were in the mood for meeting people. I don't know about Kierkegaard as someone to meet. I don't think I'm in the same league, but I might be in the same league as Nietzsche. But I don't think that I'll ever be as great as Nietzsche. I would like to feel that I'm in a peer group, where there are not many people; there's Kafka, Rilke, Holderlein. I really can't think after that. Certainly Freud has achieved more than I have so far, it seems. At a certain level there's a limitation in Freud's overall vision, however finely he's filled out the edges of his vision with his own sensibility, in a form that will flow on to the twenty-first century. He's got a limitation of vision that I feel I've got an edge on.

Me: Freud is necessarily a diminishing figure. He got it all so wrong.

Laing: He's fading isn't he?

Me: I agree that you have the edge on Freud. I feel that in a romantic sense there are eternal truths that your thinking is based upon, which are simpler than Freud's, in many ways less appealing to people who get off on intellectual formulations. But in the long run I agree.

Laing: The art of writing that is required to match simplicity is what I've got to work on. I don't think I've fully found the fulfilled, accomplished way for me to write fully to express that eternal simplicity. But I don't feel it's impossible for me to do that.

References

Introduction
1. Anthony Storr, *The Divided Legacy of R. D. Laing*, Sunday Times, 27 September 1989.
2. Colin Wilson, *Lord of the Underworld*, p.9. Aquarian Press, 1984.
3. Storr, op. cit.
4. Plato, *The Last Days of Socrates*, p.53. Penguin Classics, 1976.

Chapter One
1. J. D. Flan, *Matisse on Art*, p.31. Phaidon Press, 1978.
2. D. Blum, *Casals and the Art of Interpretation*, p.1. Heinemann, 1977.
3. Soetsu Yanagi, *The Unknown Craftsman*, p.109. Edited by B. Leach, Kudasha International, 1978.
4. Blum, op. cit., p.210.
5. R. D. Laing, *The Divided Self*, p.34. Penguin, 1969.
6. Ibid p.165.
7. Leonard Bernstein, *Findings*, p.138. Macdonald, 1982.
8. *The Laughing Man*. Vol 15 No 2, 1984.
9. *Collected Works of C G Jung*, Vol 16. p.72. Routledge and Kegan Paul.
10. R. D. Laing, *The Politics of Experience*, p.39. Penguin, 1981.
11. Eknath Easwaran, *Gandhi The Man*, p.114. Turnstone Press, 1983.

Chapter Two
1. C. G. Jung, *Memories, Dreams and Reflections*, p.194. Fontana, 1963.

2. Alfred Reynolds, *Pilates Question*, p.15. The London Letter, 1964.
3. Lao Tzu, Tao Te Ching, p.57. Penguin Classics, 1963.
4. Sigmund Freud, *Introductory Lectures on Psychoanalysis*, p.194. Vol V Parts I and II.
5. Ann Faraday, *Dream Power*, p.99. Pan, 1977.
6. Freud, op. cit., p.114.
7. Gerhard Adler ed, *C. G. Jung Letters*, Vol 1. p.57. Routledge and Kegan Paul, 1973.
8. Vaihinger, *The Philosophy of 'As If'*, p.19. Routledge and Kegan Paul, 1935.
9. Ibid., p.xlvi
10. Plato, *The Last Days of Socrates*, p.52. Penguin Classics, 1976

Chapter Three
1. Nietzsche, *Twilight of The Idols*, p.25. Penguin Classics, 1968.
2. Nietzsche, *Thus Spake Zarathustra*, p.148. Penguin Classics, 1969.
3. Ibid., p.148.
4. Soshitsu Sen XV, *Tea Life, Tea Mind*, p.11. Weatherhill, 1979.
5. P. L. Evans, *R. D. Laing The Man and His Ideas*, p.l. Dutton, 1976.
6. Barbara Hannah, *Jung – His Life and Work*, p.128. Michael Joseph, 1977.
7. Evans, op. cit., p.li.
8. Donald Meltzer, *The Kleinian Development*, Roland Harris Educational Trust.
9. R. D. Laing, *Wisdom, Folly and Madness*, p.141. Macmillan, 1985.
10. Ibid., p.143.
11. Laurens Van der Post, *A Walk With a White Bushman*, p.513. Penguin, 1987.
12. Hannah, op. cit., p.130. (see note 6)

13. Bernard Leach, *Hamada, Potter*, p.95. Kodansha International, 1975.
14. Susan Peterson, *Shoji Hamada. A Potter's Way and Work*, p.189. Kodansha International, 1975.
15. Okakura Kakurgo, *The Book of Tea*, p.110. Charles Tuttle, 1956. (Quoting Rikiu.)
16. Soetsu Yanagi, *The Unknown Craftsman*, p.191. Kudasha International, 1978.
17. Ibid., op. cit., p.9.
18. Easwaran, op. cit., p.114.
19. Leach, op. cit., p.79.
20. Ibid., p.89.
21. Ibid., p.99.
22. C. G. Jung, *Memories Dreams and Reflections*, p.338. Fontana, 1961
23. Ibid., p.392.

Chapter Four
1. Miguel Serrano, *C G Jung and Herman Hesse – A Record of Two Friendships*, p.3. Routledge and Kegan Paul, 1966.
2. Ibid., pp.90–91.
3. Reynolds, op. cit., p.18.
4. Ibid., p.4.
5. Ibid., p.4.
6. Ibid., p.5.
7. Radmila Moacanin, *Jung's Psychology and Tibetan Buddhism*, p.5. Wisdom Publications, 1986.
8. R. D. Laing, *The Politics of Experience*, p.35. Penguin, 1967.
9. Ibid., p.47.

Chapter Five
1. Richard Bach, *Illusions*, p.47. Pan, 1978.
2. R. D. Laing, *Self and Others*, p.75. Penguin, 1969.
3. C. G. Jung, *The Practice of Psychotherapy, Collected Works*, Vol XVI, p.116. Routledge and Kegan Paul, 1976.
4. Bob Deveraux, *Be Green*, Ark Press, 1975.
5. Bernard Leach, *Beyond East and West*, p.166. Faber and Faber, 1978.

6. Bruno Bettelheim, *The Informed Heart*, p.12. Penguin, 1986.

Chapter Six

1. Joscelyn Godwin, *Mystery Religions in the Ancient World*, p.34. Thames and Hudson, 1981
2. Ward Rutherford, *Celtic Mythology*, p.110. Aquarian Press, 1987.
3. Anne Ross and Don Robins, *The Life and Death of a Druid Prince*, p.132. Century Hutchinson, 1989.
4. Sigmund Freud, *Introductory Lectures*, *Vol XV. The Standard Edition of the Complete Works of Sigmund Freud*, p.142. Hogarth Press, 1961.
5. Ward Rutherford, *The Druids*, p.60. Aquarian Press, 1983.
6. R. D. Laing, *The Politics of Experience*, p.115. Penguin, 1967.
7. Rutherford, op. cit., p.59.
8. Francis Huxley, *The Guardian*, 25 August 1989.
9. Ward Rutherford, *Celtic Mythology*, p.100. Aquarian Press, 1987.
10. Neville Drury, *The Elements of Shamanism*, p.32. Element Books, 1989.
11. Evans, op. cit., p.21.
12. Laing, op. cit., p.114.
13. R. D. Laing, *The Voice of Experience*, p.156. Allen, 1982.
14. Ibid., p.49.
15. Andrew Collier, *R D Laing – The Philosophy and Politics of Psychotherapy*, p.1. Harvester Press, 1977.
16. Laing, op. cit., p.169.
17. Lao Tzu, *Tao Te Ching*, translated by Gia-Fu Feng and Jane English, Chapter 47. Wildwood House, 1984.

Chapter Seven

1. Marie Louise Von Franz, *C. G. Jung – His Myth in Our Time*, p.99. C. G. Jung Foundation, 1975.
2. Ibid., p.101.
3. Ibid., p.105.
4. Ibid., p.106.

5. Ibid., p.263.
6. Ibid., p.99.
7. Ibid., p.262.
8. Bernard Leach, *Dramas, Verse and Belief,* Jupiter Books, 1977 (Permission to quote from the author).

Coda
1. Richard Bach, *Illusions,* p.48. Pan, 1977.
2. Nietzsche, *Beyond Good and Evil,* p.89. Penguin Classics, 1973.

Coda

Richard Bach wrote in *Illusions*:-

You
teach best
what you most need
to learn[1]

I certainly needed to learn what I have written in this book.
As you will have discovered though, I am not a writer. Like
Leach, 'I am content with just adequate skill to embody living
thought.'

I anticipate a lot of opposition to what I have written.
But as Nietzsche wrote, 'I do not like it' – 'Why?' – 'I am not
up to it.' – 'Has anyone ever answered like that?'[2]

My most recent psychic experience:- On 11 July, four
days before I met Ronnie Laing for the last time, I dreamed
that I was talking about him to a lady dressed in black. I was
very upset whenever I mentioned Ronnie.

I couldn't understand why I would have such a dream
when I was so looking forward to seeing him again.

Index